101 468 123 5

Rights, Welfare, and
Mill's Moral Theory

D0303280

ONE WEEK LOAN

05 MAY 2000

23-3-04

22 SEP 2000

15 MAR 2001

25 MAY 2001

04 DEC 2001

18 DEC 2001

- 4 MAR 2002

15 DEC 2003

998

98

199

18 FEB 1999

18 NOV 1999

06 MAY 1999

05 MAY 2000

Rights, Welfare, and Mill's Moral Theory

DAVID LYONS

New York   Oxford
OXFORD UNIVERSITY PRESS
1994

Oxford University Press

Oxford   New York   Toronto
Delhi   Bombay   Calcutta   Madras   Karachi
Kuala Lumpur   Singapore   Hong Kong   Tokyo
Nairobi   Dar es Salaam   Cape Town
Melbourne   Auckland   Madrid

and associated companies in
Berlin   Ibadan

Copyright © 1994 by Oxford University Press, Inc.

Published by Oxford University Press, Inc.
200 Madison Avenue, New York, New York 10016

Oxford is a registered trademark of Oxford University Press

All rights reserved. No part of this publication may be reproduced,
stored in a retrieval system, or transmitted, in any form or by any means,
electronic, mechanical, photocopying, recording, or otherwise,
without the prior permission of Oxford University Press

Library of Congress Cataloging-in-Publication Data
Lyons, David, 1935–
Rights, welfare, and Mill's moral theory / David Lyons.
p.   cm.
Includes bibliographical references and index.
ISBN 0–19–508217–6; ISBN 0–19–508218–4 (pbk.)
1. Mill, John Stuart, 1806–1873.   2. Ethics, Modern—19th century.
3. Utilitarianism.   I. Title.
B1608.E8L96   1994   171′.5′092—dc20   93–34799

SHEFFIELD HALLAM UNIVERSITY LIBRARY
WL
171·5
LY
COLLEGIATE CRESCENT

9 8 7 6 5 4 3 2 1

Printed in the United States of America
on acid-free paper

To the memory of
HERBERT HART

Preface

Max Black first suggested that I look into the subject of rights. Joel Feinberg, William Frankena, and Herbert Hart were kind enough to recommend readings. My explorations led to essay 1, into legal theory, and to a study of Bentham.

When I completed the latter, *A Theory of Justice,* by John Rawls, appeared. Some commentators welcomed that enormously important book by writing epitaphs for utilitarianism. I found that puzzling. To my knowledge, there had been nothing like a rigorous study of the possible relations between justice and utilitarianism.

Mill's work seemed a place to begin work on those issues, for Mill took them seriously and in his essay *Utilitarianism* proposed an accommodation. It remained undeveloped, perhaps because of the received wisdom that Mill was an *act-utilitarian*.

My work on Bentham made me familiar with Mill's commentaries, which suggested a way to reconstruct his theory of justice. Essays 2 through 6 are the outcome of that project. Like my earlier work on utilitarianism, they apply analytical methods in an attempt to understand controversies in normative ethics.

Scholarly work published since these essays began to appear testify to renewed interest in Mill and increasing interest in the relations between rights and utilitarianism. The state of the literature suggests that my essays may still contribute to an understanding of those issues.

I am grateful to the National Endowment for the Humanities, the Cornell Law School, and the College of Arts and Sciences of Cornell University for supporting work on this volume; to Angela Blackburn and Rob Dilworth at Oxford University Press for aid and encouragement; to Thaddeus Metz for help with the Introduction; to Carol Roberts for the Index; and to Jennifer Cammarata for help with the manuscript.

Like many others, I first encountered Herbert Hart by reading his *Concept of Law*. I had the good fortune to meet Hart personally, to attend his lectures in Oxford, and even to receive comments from him on my work. Like many others, I soon realized I was in touch with a great, gifted, gentle, and generous human being.

Hart was my supervisor during a postdoctoral year in Oxford thirty years ago. His help and hospitality were supererogatory. We met only occasionally thereafter—in London, Oxford, Jerusalem. I had the privilege of visiting Hart during his last spring in Oxford and of securing his permission to dedicate this volume to him.

Ithaca, New York   D.B.L.
July 1993

Acknowledgments

Essay 1. "Rights, Claimants, and Beneficiaries," *American Philosophical Quarterly* 6(1969): 173–85. Reprinted with permission.

Essay 2. "Mill's Theory of Morality," *Noûs* 10(1976): 101–20. Reprinted with permission.

Essay 3. "Mill's Theory of Justice," in *Values and Morals: Essays in Honor of William Frankena, Charles Stevenson, and Richard Brandt,* ed. A. I. Goldman and J. Kim, pp. 1–20. (Dordrecht: Reidel, 1978). Copyright © 1978 by D. Reidel Publishing Company, Dordrecht, Holland. Reprinted by permission of Kluwer Academic Publishers.

Essay 4. "Liberty and Harm to Others," in *New Essays on John Stuart Mill and Utilitarianism,* ed. W. E. Cooper, K. Nielsen, and S. C. Patten, *Canadian Journal of Philosophy Suppl.* 5(1979): 1–19. Reprinted with permission.

Essay 5. "Benevolence and Justice in Mill," in *The Limits of Utilitarianism,* ed. H. Miller and W. H. Williams, pp. 42–70 (Minneapolis: University of Minnesota Press, 1982). Copyright © 1982 by the University of Minnesota. Reprinted by permission of the University of Minnesota Press.

Essay 6. "Utility and Rights," in *Ethics, Economics, and the Law: Nomos XXIV,* ed. J. R. Pennock and J. W. Chapman, pp. 107–38 (New York: New York University Press, 1982). Reprinted with permission.

The essays are reproduced here with minor changes.

Contents

Abbreviations

UT = John Stuart Mill, *Utilitarianism* (1861).
OL = John Stuart Mill, *On Liberty* (1859).

Unless otherwise noted, parenthetical references in the text are to these works. As they are available in many editions, the references cite chapters and paragraphs, using uppercase Roman and Arabic numerals, respectively. Thus, *"UT* V, 14" refers to *Utilitarianism,* chapter 5, paragraph 14.

The new standard editions are in *The Collected Works of John Stuart Mill,* ed. John M. Robson (Toronto: University of Toronto Press, 1969, 1977), 10:203–59, 18:213–310.

Rights, Welfare, and
Mill's Moral Theory

Introduction

Rights play a leading role in moral thinking but present puzzles to moral theory: What is it to have a right? Are rights compatible with steadfast service of the general welfare? The essays collected in this volume address those issues.

These essays take as their starting points the work of three theorists: Jeremy Bentham, Herbert Hart, and John Stuart Mill. Like Mill and Hart, I assume that we have moral as well as legal rights.[1] Some reject this notion, so section I comments on that issue. The remainder of the Introduction relates the arguments of the essays to developments in the philosophical literature.

I. Moral Rights

If I carelessly cause you harm, I not only act wrongly but wrong you. We might explain this as follows: I owe it to others to take reasonable care not to cause them harm; in being negligent, I have failed to meet that responsibility. It seems to follow that I have violated your right that others shall take reasonable care not to cause you harm.

Moral rights (in the relevant sense) are rights whose existence depends on principle and fact, not on social recognition or enforcement. Some doubt that you can have a right if it is not enforceable by law. This

---

1. Like them, I assume, too, that we can have morally defensible legal rights—rights whose moral force depends not on their legal status but on their moral defensibility. See essay 6.

is puzzling, because comparable skepticism about moral requirements is rare. Few, if any, theorists suggest that duties or obligations are fictitious unless they are enforceable. To compound the puzzle, some moral requirements go hand in hand with rights.

A skeptic might suggest that moral rights are superfluous conceptions, perhaps even figments of our imagination, because we can translate talk about rights into less problematic talk about moral requirements. But that inference, too, is puzzling. In the first place, the idea of a moral right seems no more problematic than that of a moral requirement. In the second place, if moral obligations were initially less problematic than rights, and judgments about the latter could be translated into judgments about the former, that fact would seem to vindicate confidence in moral rights.

For present purposes, let us consider a less abstract aspect of our example. If I have carelessly caused you harm, I am bound in good conscience to compensate you for the injury that I have wrongfully done to you. In other words, I owe you compensation. But if that's true, then it seems undeniable that you have a right to recompense. It does not matter whether your right to compensation is recognized by law.

Your right does not mean merely that you could properly accept compensation, should it be offered. You have a legitimate claim to compensation, provision of which would be neither gratuitous nor supererogatory. If recompense is not forthcoming, you will suffer a second wrong. Resentment or indignation will be all the more appropriate.

In brief, if moral considerations imply that I owe you something, then there seems no reason to deny that you have a moral right to it from me. The idea of a right is at home among our moral concepts.

In the case we are imagining, your right results from my negligence, which created a new moral relationship between us. You have a basis in fact and principle for pressing a claim against me—not in a court of law, perhaps, but in the court of conscience. Of course, you can also waive the right and decline compensation.

This matter concerns the two of us directly, other persons less directly (if at all). Some others may be familiar enough with the circumstances to make sound moral judgments about your right and my obligation. But unless you have engaged someone to act on your behalf, you alone retain the moral authority to press or waive your claim against me.

This case exemplifies the "personal" aspect of morality that was stressed by Ross some sixty years ago.[2] Ross noted that rights go hand in hand with moral requirements.[3] Some of the requirements listed by Ross (e.g., the duty to promote justice) presuppose no special relationship between individuals, but others do, as in our example.

Ross gave brief notice to moral rights. Like other theorists of his time, he focused on moral requirements. Nevertheless, the attention that he gave to rights was exceptional for a moral theorist during the first half of the twentieth century.

The second half of this century, by contrast, has been a time of rights consciousness. That development within the scholarly community reflects social and political movements outside it—movements against governmental acts such as genocide and social structures such as institutionalized racism, which are understood to violate human rights.

Some theorists are made unhappy by talk of human rights. This attitude is not new. The same was true two centuries ago, when Bentham attacked the idea of natural rights.[4]

Although Bentham attacked the idea of natural rights, his analytical theories excluded moral rights generally; for he held that rights presuppose duties and that duties are creatures of the law alone.[5] As my example of the right to compensation suggests, however, unproblematic moral considerations, by themselves alone, appear to imply some moral rights.

Some theorists have objected not to the idea of moral rights generally but to the notion of human rights specifically, because they are called "natural" and declarations of them have been described as "self-evident." But the idea of a human right need not be burdened by such problematic notions. The idea, after all, is that some moral rights are not based on special relationships between particular individuals.

2. W. D. Ross, *The Right and the Good* (Oxford: Clarendon, 1930), esp. chap. 2 and app.

3. Writers frequently call the requirements that correlate with rights "obligations," but the differences among the species of moral requirements do not matter here.

4. Jeremy Bentham, "Anarchical Fallacies," in *The Works of Jeremy Bentham,* ed. J. Bowring, 2: 489–534 (Edinburgh: Tait, 1838–43).

5. Bentham held that duties were created by coercive commands. Although he recognized extralegal sanctions, he seems not to have considered that coercive commands might create duties and therefore rights outside the law. These would not be moral rights or duties in the relevant sense, however, for they would presuppose widespread recognition and some sort of enforcement, however informal that might be. Bentham's utilitarianism would seem independently to exclude moral rights; see essay 6.

Human rights are moral rights that are possessed unconditionally by all persons.

Some theorists worry that rights decline in value when claimed as widely as they are today. These concerns may be occasioned by calls for aid on behalf of disadvantaged people throughout the world—not as charity to be dispensed at our discretion but as rights that demand respect.

Sometimes, worries about claims to aid may simply express the resistance of privileged parties to the loss of economic advantages. But that is not always the case. People in relatively affluent communities may honestly wonder how they could possibly meet the pressing needs of so many millions around the world. They may assume that rights to aid can truly be said to exist only if all of the relevant needs can be met by direct assistance on the part of other individuals acting separately to discharge their corresponding moral obligations. This overlooks the possibility that one might be morally bound to work for collective action in one's own political community. (As mobilizations for war too often demonstrate, collective action can overcome enormous obstacles.) In other words, a right to aid may correlate with others' obligations to act for effective measures that would provide aid.

Other worries about moral rights represent deep divisions within substantive moral and political theory. They derive from the fact that some theories have seemed incompatible with the role of rights in moral judgment. If we have moral rights, which are independent of law, we can appraise law accordingly. If law fails that test, we can legitimately demand reform or more radical change. Asking whether the law of the land respects moral rights is different from asking whether, for example, the law promotes the general welfare. The results of those two tests might differ. Some believe that law need only serve the general welfare—that when law does so, it achieves all that morality requires. Such a theorist should indeed reject moral rights—unless she thinks that rights are somehow grounded on, and subordinate to, service of the general welfare.

Those substantive problems provide the background for the central issues in this volume. They are the concerns of essays 2 through 6.

II. Rights and Beneficiaries

Anticipating philosophical developments of this century, Bentham maintained that we should not ask what a right is. He held that rights are not real entities because we cannot conceivably inspect them. To understand rights, we should translate the ascription of a right into more basic terms. We can understand talk of rights by asking what difference it makes, in real terms, to have one.

Bentham's analysis proceeded as follows. He held that coercive commands and prohibitions are the building blocks of law; that they create legal duties and obligations; that statements ascribing legal rights can be translated into statements ascribing legal duties or obligations to others;[6] and that legal rights arise specifically when legal duties or obligations are beneficial.[7]

In his inaugural lecture, Hart endorsed the idea of analyzing rights by identifying their grounds.[8] Hart agreed that duties and obligations are fundamental features of law and more basic than the legal rights with which they are associated.[9] But he rejected the notion that rights should be analyzed in terms of beneficial obligations.

It seems an inherent feature of rights that they are advantageous to their owners. Bentham explained this by suggesting that rights accrue to those who are likely to benefit—or who stand to benefit—from others' performance of their obligations. In his British Academy lecture on Bentham, Hart criticized that view.[10] He suggested that what is distinctive and important about rights is the control that having a right gives one over others' freedom.

The first essay in this volume was written as a response to Hart's initial critique of Bentham's theory of rights. It suggests that the *beneficiary theory* should be understood as holding that rights belong to those who are *supposed* to benefit from others' dutiful conduct, not to those who merely stand to benefit. This *qualified beneficiary theory* is more plausible than the unqualified theory considered by Hart, seems less

6. The literature assumes that legal prohibitions and requirements are duties or obligations. This creates problems if duties and obligations necessarily have moral force but legal requirements do not; see my review of *H.L.A. Hart,* by Neil MacCormick, *Cornell Law Review* 68(1983): 257–68.

7. Another kind of right acknowledged by Bentham is the absence of a coercive restriction. Such rights can be beneficial, but Bentham's theory does not cover them.

8. H.L.A. Hart, *Definition and Theory in Jurisprudence* (Oxford: Clarendon, 1953).

9. Hart does not agree with Bentham that law is reducible to requirements and prohibitions, on the ground that legal powers are not reducible to restrictions; see his *Concept of Law* (Oxford: Clarendon, 1961), chap. 3.

10. Hart, "Bentham: Lecture on a Master Mind," *Proceedings of the British Academy* 48(1962): 297–320.

vulnerable to objections, and appears to account for more rights than does Hart's proposal.

In a subsequent paper, Hart focused on rights that are conferred by law. He emphasized the views of legal theorists and the interests that lawyers have in talking about rights. Redirecting his critique so that it bears upon the qualified beneficiary theory, Hart argued that being the intended beneficiary of a legal duty is neither necessary nor sufficient for having a legal right: some persons who are supposed to benefit from the performance of legal obligations are not on that account regarded as having rights (at least by legal theorists), and some who are regarded as having rights are not the intended beneficiaries of legal requirements.[11] Hart also developed further his alternative theory, which centers on "legally respected individual choice." He argued that this conception of what it is to have a legal right best covers paradigm cases of rights in "ordinary" law.[12]

Hart drew attention to the distinction between private law (where the enforcement of legal requirements is left to the discretion of persons who are regarded as having legal rights) and criminal law (where legal requirements are enforced by officials). Because some prohibitions in the criminal law are meant to safeguard interests of individuals, the beneficiary theory understands them as conferring rights. Because duties under the criminal law cannot be waived or enforced by those whose interests they are meant to serve, the *choice theory* implies that criminal law prohibitions do *not* confer rights. Hart saw this contrast as a reason to prefer the choice theory. He believed that rights should not be said to arise when duties are merely beneficial. Such talk would devalue rights: it would render them redundant or useless, of no special interest to lawyers or legal theorists.[13]

Hart conceded that his choice theory does not account for some rights of importance to law, such as rights that cannot be waived but that are regarded as fundamental in a legal system, as well as rights that contribute to the moral appraisal of law. Hart did not regard these as counterexamples to the choice theory. He suggested, rather, that they illustrate

11. Hart, "Bentham on Legal Rights," in *Oxford Essays in Jurisprudence: Second Series,* ed. A. W. B. Simpson, pp. 171–201 (Oxford: Clarendon, 1973). This essay is also published as "Legal Rights" in Hart's *Essays on Bentham,* pp. 162–93 (Oxford: Clarendon, 1982).

12. Hart, "Bentham on Legal Rights," p. 201.

13. Hart, "Bentham on Legal Rights," p. 182.

the limited capacity of general theories to accommodate the complexity of law.

After Hart's essay on legal rights appeared, other theorists joined the controversy. A few developments might be mentioned here. Hart had suggested a link between the beneficiary theory and utilitarianism.[14] The association is natural. Bentham provides a historical basis for it, and a beneficiary theory could also be attributed to Mill. Furthermore, utilitarianism is concerned with the service of interests, and the protection of interests is the focus of the beneficiary theory.[15] Wayne Sumner shows, however, that the theory's link with utilitarianism is historical, not conceptual. Sumner combines a utilitarian theory with a choice conception of rights like Hart's.[16]

In his defense of a beneficiary theory, Neil MacCormick notes that constitutional and criminal law provisions protect interests all the more securely because the rights they create cannot be waived. MacCormick holds that such cases undermine Hart's choice theory and support a beneficiary theory.

MacCormick also responds to Hart's argument that redundancy threatens rights when they are construed as the beneficiary theory construes them. This assumes that duties are more basic than rights. MacCormick argues, on the contrary, that ascriptions of rights cannot be "reduced" to judgments about beneficial duties because the former are often more basic than the latter.[17]

MacCormick suggests a modification of the beneficiary theory. The unqualified theory counts someone as having a right who merely stands to benefit—or is likely to benefit—from another's dutiful conduct. The problem with this analysis is that someone who lacks a relevant right can stand to benefit from dutiful conduct merely coincidentally, not by virtue of having any relevant right.

Suppose, for example, that you would like to give a gift to someone (a

14. This is suggested in "Bentham on Legal Rights," pp. 183, 193. Hart similarly emphasized the "utilitarian" origins of legal positivism, although he seemed to appreciate that the linkage is historical, not conceptual; see his "Positivism and the Separation of Law and Morals," *Harvard Law Review* 761(1958): 593–629.

15. Of course, the generic theory known as *consequentialism* would not focus exclusively (if at all) on interests.

16. L. W. Sumner, *The Moral Foundation of Rights* (Oxford: Clarendon, 1987).

17. D. N. MacCormick, "Rights in Legislation," in *Law, Morality, and Society,* ed. P. M. S. Hacker and J. Raz, pp. 189–209 (Oxford: Clarendon, 1977).

third party) but will be able to afford the gift if and only if I repay a loan that I owe you. The third party stands to benefit from my dutiful conduct but lacks a relevant right. The third party may well have the right to accept a gift from you, in the sense that it would not be improper to do so, but that right is independent of my duty to repay you. In this sort of case, you have the relevant right. Thus, the unqualified beneficiary theory has some false implications.

The qualified theory avoids this problem by claiming that one has a right if and only if one does not merely stand to benefit but is supposed to benefit from another's dutiful conduct. The right holder is an intended (not a merely coincidental) beneficiary.[18] In this respect, the qualified beneficiary theory links benefits very tightly to dutiful conduct.

MacCormick suggests a looser connection between rights and benefits. He holds that, when a statute confers the right to something, possession of that thing is not necessarily a good for each and every person who qualifies as having the right but is a good for such persons "normally."[19]

Another loose but important connection between rights and benefits has been suggested by Joseph Raz.[20] Raz holds that some rights are more basic than the duties with which they are linked. He speaks of rights and duties "protecting" interests, of interests "grounding" rights, and of rights "grounding" duties. These metaphors merit explication.

Raz contends that the linkage between rights, duties, and interests is justificatory, not conceptual. One can support the attribution of some duties by citing rights, and one can justify the ascription of a right, in turn, by citing an important interest. The performance of duties that are so grounded is supposed to serve those interests. The derived duties are variable, for how one must act so as to protect a relevant interest can change with circumstances.

One of the important claims made by Raz is that, although rights and duties turn on interests, some rights do not rest directly on the relevant interests. One can justify the ascription of "derivative" rights by show-

18. The crucial condition (that the right holder is supposed to benefit) implies that some interest of the right holder is or would be served by performance of a duty, but it does not imply that the right holder does or would benefit overall. The dutiful conduct might lead the right holder to suffer a greater loss.

19. MacCormick, "Rights in Legislation," p. 204.

20. Joseph Raz, *The Morality of Freedom* (Oxford: Clarendon, 1986), chap. 7.

ing that respecting them is conducive to respecting more basic rights. The relevant interests are those that ground the basic, "core" rights. On this view, interests are connected closely with core rights but not so closely with derivative rights and duties.

A differently innovative approach to rights builds upon W. N. Hohfeld's influential classification scheme for rights.[21] Hohfeld believed that lawyers sometimes draw erroneous inferences about the law because they fail to make relevant distinctions among the various kinds of rights. He held that there are four elemental types of legal rights:

1. A *claim-right* belonging to one person implies and is implied by a duty, belonging to another person, that is owed to the first. An example is your right against me to be repaid what you loaned me.
2. A *liberty* is equivalent to the absence of a duty owed to another party,[22] as when a property owner permits me to cross his or her land and exempts me from the duty not to trespass.
3. A *power* is a capability, conferred by law, to change someone's legal condition (e.g., my capacity to contract), exercise of which generates rights and obligations.
4. An *immunity* is the absence of vulnerability to some change in one's legal condition. I have an immunity when, for example, another is not empowered to dispose of my property without my authorization.

Carl Wellman argues that Hohfeld's categories do not collect rights consistently.[23] For example, it seems implausible to regard all Hohfeldian immunities as rights. According to Hohfeld's definitions, one has an immunity if one is prevented by law from inheriting property. But being legally barred from inheriting property hardly seems to qualify as a right. Wellman also observes that the rights collected in Hohfeldian categories are not equally simple and equally elemental. One with a claim-right is empowered to enforce or waive another's correlative

21. Wesley Newcomb Hohfeld, *Fundamental Legal Conceptions,* ed. W. W. Cook (New Haven: Yale University Press, 1964). My summary substitutes "claim-right" and "liberty" for Hohfeld's "claim" and "privilege."

22. In Hohfeld's scheme each elemental right involves a relation with another individual. Thus a liberty is not the general absence of a restriction on one's conduct but is equivalent to not owing a particular duty to some other individual.

23. Carl Wellman, *A Theory of Rights* (Totowa, N.J.: Rowman & Allanheld, 1985).

obligation, but this means that a claim-right includes a power as a proper constituent part.

Wellman's criticisms are important because moral philosophers who become aware of Hohfeld's scheme can be so impressed by its good sense and theoretically pleasing symmetries that they may uncritically assume it to be sound and then suppose that a parallel scheme applies unproblematically to moral rights.

Wellman does not totally reject Hohfeld's categories. He contends, rather, that full-fledged rights are composites of Hohfeldian elements. The Hohfeldian ''core'' of a right determines its content, and ''associated'' Hohfeldian elements ''contribute some measure of freedom or control directly.''

Wellman also proposes a ''confrontation model'' of rights. Like beneficiary theorists, he regards rights as advantages; but the kind of advantage that Wellman believes rights provide reflects the choice theory: ''Rights concern the distribution of freedom [and control] to the rightholder . . . in some possible confrontation of wills.''[24] The competition between choice and beneficiary theories of rights remains far from settled.

III. Mill on Rights and Welfare

Most of the essays in this volume explore the relations between rights and utilitarian principles. Essays 2–5 do so by interpreting Mill's most directly relevant views. Essay 6 reflects critically on the possibility of a utilitarian theory of rights.

These essays were occasioned by the publication of John Rawls's *A Theory of Justice*.[25] That book fully merits the enthusiastic reception it received. However, some reviews did not merely celebrate the profound contributions made by Rawls but proclaimed that utilitarianism had finally been routed. That was premature. The possibility of a utilitarian theory of justice had hardly been explored in the philosophical literature.

The blame falls partly on utilitarian theorists, who have neglected the clear challenge presented by our commonplace uses of the concept of justice. Some utilitarians have evaded that challenge by embracing the

24. Wellman, *Theory of Rights,* p. 93.
25. John Rawls, *A Theory of Justice* (Cambridge, Mass.: Belknap, 1971).

notion that justice is basically "formal"—that it consists in the uniform treatment of cases.[26] That is implausible. Justice requires some kind of uniformity but is surely more than just abiding by rules regardless of their contents or merits. No kind of justice would be done by uniformly rewarding rapists and punishing Good Samaritans. It is sometimes suggested that *administrative justice,* required when applying rules to particular cases, consists in their uniform treatment.[27] Even in that sphere, however, the notion of "formal" justice seems inadequate.[28]

As Mill was the one great utilitarian theorist to confront the seeming conflict between justice and utility and to sketch a utilitarian approach to justice, his theory seems a natural place to begin. The project was not encouraged by the secondary literature. Mill is usually considered an act-utilitarian—that is, as holding that morality basically requires each of us always to act so as to promote happiness or welfare as much as possible. For reasons I shall give, that moral theory does not seem compatible with a plausible conception of justice.

The conventional reading of Mill was challenged by Urmson, who noted the importance placed by Mill on moral rules and obligations.[29] Although Urmson's revisionism was not widely accepted, Mill's comments on the nature of justice and morality suggested that a stronger case could be developed for a reading that held out some promise of reconciling justice with utilitarianism.

Essays 2 through 5 present the results of that inquiry by offering a new interpretation of Mill's approach to moral theory. Essays 2 and 3 reconstruct his theories of moral right and justice, respectively; essay 5 delves further into the complexities of those theories.

Before commenting on the argument of those essays, I should say something about essay 4, which offers a new reading of Mill's principle of liberty (sometimes called the *harm principle*). Although related to the other interpretive claims, the thesis of essay 4 is also somewhat independent of them.

Mill argues that freedom may be limited only for the sake of harm prevention. His principle is usually understood to condone interference only with conduct that threatens to harm others. Essay 4 argues, on both

26. Or they evade it by embracing the vaguer notion that justice consists in treating like cases alike.

27. For this view, see Hart, *Concept of Law,* pp. 153–57.

28. See David Lyons, "On Formal Justice," *Cornell Law Review* 58(1973): 833–61.

29. See the first paragraph of essay 2 for references to the earlier literature.

textual and philosophical grounds, that the principle approves interference when it serves the purpose of preventing harm to other persons.
As Mill seemed to recognize, harm to others can sometimes be prevented indirectly, by interfering with behavior that itself would not
cause harm to others. For better or worse, this widens the scope of
justifiable interference and makes available harm prevention measures
that the principle as usually understood would prohibit.

Essays 2, 3, and 5 base their interpretation of Mill on his explicitly
analytical remarks in the last chapter of *Utilitarianism*. They argue that
Mill commits himself to the following propositions as partial elucida-
tions of central moral concepts: an act is morally wrong if and only if
it violates a moral obligation: moral principles determine obligations
and thereby determine how one should behave; a subset of moral
principles—the requirements of justice—do that and more: they also
imply that other persons have rights. Someone has a right just when he
has "a sufficient claim, on whatever account, to have something guaranteed to him by society" (*UT* V, 24). To these analytical propositions
Mill adds the substantive moral claim that "no other reason" can be
given to support the ascription of a moral right "than general utility"
(ibid.). This reflects his utilitarianism.

Thus, Mill understands justice in terms of moral rights. That understanding is plausible, and it is widely accepted by moral theorists.[30] But
Mill's analytical remarks about moral rights are vague, and his utilitarian account of rights is vaguer. His position calls for reconstructive
interpretation.

The original aim of these essays was not to construct a definitive
scholarly interpretation of Mill but to identify a promising utilitarian
approach to moral rights and justice. The reading of Mill that is offered
here seeks primarily to serve that aim by addressing two problems for a
utilitarian theory of rights. One is the *grounding problem*—how to base
moral rights on a utilitarian theory. Moral theorists have usually understood utilitarianism to require that one always promote welfare as much
as possible. Such a principle gives no hint of how to support an assertion
that some individual has a moral right. The other is the *trumping problem*. It seems part of our very notion of a moral right that rights make a
principled difference to the determination of right and wrong conduct. In
this respect, rights resemble obligations, which present a similar prob-

---

30. In essay 3 I question this view of the relation between justice and rights.

lem for utilitarian theory. The difficulty can be sketched as follows. Act-utilitarianism is regarded by many theorists (critics and champions alike) as the principle that most faithfully represents the utilitarian approach to morality. It holds that welfare maximization is the necessary and sufficient condition of right conduct, that is, that the rightness of conduct is determined solely by the marginal utility of particular acts.[31] This implies that welfare maximization is a sufficient justification for infringing a right, which means that rights can make no principled difference to the morality of conduct. For these reasons, respecting rights seems incompatible with act-utilitarianism and thus with the utilitarian tradition.

It has become customary to refer to the relevant feature of rights by saying that they "trump" minimal welfare considerations.[32] That expression has proved to be misleading: it suggests that rights always take precedence over welfare considerations. But neither rights nor obligations are normally conceived of as "absolute." We assume that they can sometimes justifiably be infringed—out of respect for conflicting rights or obligations that are more stringent in the circumstances, in order to prevent great harm, and perhaps even to secure great gains.[33] But the infringement of a right cannot generally be justified by the mere fact that it would promote welfare minimally more than would respecting the right.

To put the matter differently, rights entail what Joseph Raz calls "exclusionary reasons"—second-order reasons for excluding from consideration otherwise valid reasons for action. Rights are not peculiarly exclusionary. Obligations, decisions, and authoritative rules, for example, can function in that way.[34]

If the only true version of utilitarianism were act-utilitarianism, the trumping problem would be insoluble. The essays in this volume reject that understanding of the tradition. They assume that a theory can qualify as utilitarian even if it is not equivalent to act-utilitarianism. Mill's version of utilitarianism is of interest because it promises to solve the

31. Marginal utility may be understood in terms of actual or likely consequences.

32. The terminology was introduced by Ronald Dworkin in the title essay of *Taking Rights Seriously,* pp. 184–205 (Cambridge, Mass.: Harvard University Press, 1978).

33. Dworkin made clear that this was how he understood the "trumping" property of rights.

34. See Joseph Raz, *Practical Reason and Norms,* 2d ed. (Princeton: Princeton University Press, 1990), chap. 1 and postscript.

grounding and trumping problems. The interpretation offered here is informed by that prospect.

How might a utilitarian theory ground moral rights? One idea is to regard a statement that on the surface asserts that someone has a moral right as equivalent to the statement that a right ought to be established and enforced, perhaps by law. A utilitarian might endorse the latter claim just when social recognition and enforcement of an institutional right would promote the general welfare.[35]

Act-utilitarianism might seem to support such reasoning; but that cannot be true without qualification. Act-utilitarianism concerns individual acts and applies directly to nothing else. It does not require laws, institutional arrangements, or anything else to maximize welfare, nor could it consistently do so.

Act-utilitarianism could not generally require that laws maximize welfare, because the effects of (say) a voting act by a member of a legislative body are not equivalent to the effects attributable to the law that the vote may help to establish or maintain. An act-utilitarian legislator might believe that if enacted, a particular law would have maximally desirable effects but nevertheless vote against it because of the undesirable side effects of an affirmative vote. An act-utilitarian legislator can have only a qualified commitment to supporting laws that create or maintain the rights that it would be most useful to have.

Hart criticized this way of attempting to reconcile moral rights with utilitarianism, on the grounds that it claims that talk of moral rights is essentially misleading. To say that there is a certain moral right, it claims, is really to mean that there ought to be some other kind of right. Hart observed that moral rights are commonly appealed to as good reasons for having certain institutional arrangements and that they could not serve in that capacity if the claim that one has a moral right were reducible to—and therefore substantively identical with—the claim that there is a good reason for having such an institutional arrangement.[36]

Hart believed that Mill made this mistake, but I read Mill differently. Mill endorsed Bentham's approach to punishment. According to Bentham, punishments are authorized by legal rules that impose requirements or prohibitions. Bentham evaluated rules by considering their welfare costs and benefits. Mill suggested an extension of this account

35. See Sumner, *Moral Foundation of Rights.*
36. Hart, *Essays on Bentham,* pp. 79–104.

so that it covers moral principles. He understood "punishment" broadly enough to encompass guilt feelings (which seem essentially connected to moral convictions when applied to one's own conduct), as well as informal social sanctions (which are to some degree a natural expression of moral convictions when they are applied to others' conduct). This suggests that moral principles, including the requirements of justice, are useful social rules, breaches of which warrant external sanctions and trigger internal sanctions (guilt feelings).

Mill thus suggests an "indirect" version of utilitarianism: rights and obligations are determined by useful principles; right conduct is generally a matter of honoring obligations; and justice consists in respecting rights, that is, in honoring obligations that correlate with rights. In that sort of theory, utilitarian reasoning applies to moral principles directly but regulates conduct only indirectly.

This theory initially appears to solve both the grounding and trumping problems. As for grounding, to establish the existence of a moral right is to justify a moral principle. For a utilitarian like Mill, this is to show, roughly, that the benefits of the principle's acceptance would exceed its costs, which include internal and external sanctions. As for trumping, the theory does not allow direct utilitarian reasoning to justify infringements of rights or obligations, because it accords utilitarian reasoning *no* direct bearing on the appraisal of conduct. Useful moral principles, not marginal utility, exclusively determine what one morally ought to do.

Although Mill's moral theory is, on this reading, an "indirect" version of utilitarianism, it is more like act-utilitarianism than rule-utilitarianism in some important respects. Like the typical act-utilitarian, Mill regards his theory as the natural or necessary expression of a commitment to the promotion of welfare. By contrast, rule-utilitarian theories typically result from conscious attempts to accommodate objections by modifying utilitarianism.

An act-utilitarian typically assumes that his principle best represents the commitment involved in regarding welfare as the sole fundamental value. If the oppportunity to promote welfare provides one with a reason to so act, then the opportunity to promote welfare to a greater degree provides a stronger reason to act. The strongest reason for action is provided by the opportunity to promote welfare to the greatest degree possible in the circumstances.

Mill can be understood to agree with the act-utilitarian's premises but to reject the conclusions. Mill assumes, not implausibly, that right and wrong are functions of moral principles, that is, of moral rights and obligations. As he does not conceive of moral principles in act-utilitarian terms, his assumption effectively rules out act-utilitarianism. But his analysis of the basic moral concepts leaves room for utilitarian reasoning in appraising moral principles. Like act-utilitarianism, Mill's theory is shaped by conceptual assumptions about reasons for action and the character of moral reasoning.

By contrast, rule-utilitarianism is typically shaped not by conceptual assumptions but by substantive objections to act-utilitarianism. It is offered as an amended utilitarianism, not as the most faithful rendering of utilitarianism. As it is more freely constructed, it can of course be made to solve the trumping problem by stipulating that the marginal utility of an act shall be irrelevant to its evaluation. But that kind of theory construction is not of interest here. Before we entertain modifications of utilitarianism, we should first determine how well alternative interpretations of its basic idea can accommodate rights and justice.

Unlike rule-utilitarianism, Mill's theory does not stipulate that the marginal utility of an act is irrelevant to its evaluation. Mill's solution to the trumping problem flows from his conceptual analysis. If Mill is wrong (if the moral concepts do not imply that the marginal utility of an act is irrelevant to its appraisal), there is no reason to suppose that his theory solves that problem.

IV. Mill's Theory Revisited

As it is interpreted here, Mill's theory faces serious objections. Moral principles are to be evaluated in terms of the utility of providing sanctions for their breach. This means that they are determined in part by the utility of self-reproach. One can be morally required to behave in a certain way only if it would be useful to inculcate guilt feelings and provide for other sanctions for failing so to behave. In allowing the utility of guilt feelings to help determine right conduct, the theory seems to put the cart before the horse; for justifiable self-reproach presupposes a just judgment that one has failed to act as one should.[37] A different objection, developed in essay 6, concerns utilitarianism generally and

37. This objection was sketched in my "Human Rights and the General Welfare," *Philosophy and Public Affairs* 6(1977): 113–29.

not Mill's theory alone. On closer inspection, it looks as if a thoroughgoing utilitarianism cannot satisfy the trumping condition.

Mill's theory assumes that the moral concepts make direct utilitarian considerations irrelevant to the morality of conduct and in this sense prohibit consideration of direct utilitarian arguments within the scope of moral deliberation. A moral framework with that feature would ensure that rights are capable of trumping direct utilitarian reasons for action. But the moral concepts are not, in fact, so rigid: it is not true that one who entertains utilitarian reasons for infringing rights has fallen into conceptual confusion.

This applies to a utilitarian who appreciates the utilitarian justification of relevant moral principles or institutional rules. Such a utilitarian should be capable, for example, of recognizing that the utility of a particular law is not always threatened by departures from it. A utilitarian official would quite properly hesitate before violating a useful law, especially one that he or she is charged with administering. But such prudence would not involve being blind, on principle, to direct utilitarian reasons for unlawful conduct. Furthermore, when an official sees him- or herself as bound by an obligation to conform that trumps direct utilitarian reasons for nonconformity, this moral perception is not entailed by, but is logically independent of, personal appreciation of the utilitarian justification of the law that is under the official's charge.

This line of reasoning is not self-evidently sound, and its conclusion has not been universally accepted.[38] For example, Kent Greenawalt argues "that much less conflict exists between a utilitarian account and common moral understanding about [morally defensible] rights" than essay 6 maintains.[39] Essay 6 understates the fact that "legal rights can be tremendously weighty factors in moral deliberations for the utilitarian," so that it will often be most reasonable for an official to assume that the "enforcement of guaranteed rights . . . will more reliably promote welfare than action based upon his own fallible judgment."[40] Given an appreciation of those factors, it becomes difficult to establish

38. I mention here just a few relevant arguments. The first two works cited are comments on essay 6; for other comments, see the Bibliography for articles by Flathman, Fletcher, and Gewirth in *Ethics, Economics, and the Law.*

39. Kent Greenawalt, "Utilitarian Justifications for Observance of Legal Rights," in *Ethics, Economics, and the Law,* ed. J. R. Pennock and J. W. Chapman (New York: New York University Press, 1982), p. 139.

40. Greenawalt, "Utilitarian Justifications," p. 142.

that a thoroughgoing utilitarian would confer on rights any less respect than they deserve. That is because the trumping condition does not call for rigorous enforcement, without exception, of morally defensible rights. Essay 6 "has oversimplified the moral and legal universes in supposing that people generally acknowledge a substantial moral constraint against violation of any legal right they think is morally defensible."[41]

Richard Hare argues that defensible rights are like principles that it is useful to be firmly disposed to respect: "in all but the most extraordinary cases . . . the most *likely* way of getting the optimific [maximally useful] act is to follow our intuitions" by respecting the principles we accept, which Hare assumes are useful.[42] Hare argues, further, that if

> the utilitarian can account for the moral justification of the *institution* of legal rights, then he must at the same time grant that there is a moral duty in general to respect and enforce the rights. For to have a morally justified system of legal rights but no moral duty to enforce or respect them in particular cases would be self-defeating. In other words, the moral duty to enforce and respect is part and parcel of the "moral force" of the system itself. . . . For if people do not acknowledge a moral duty to respect and enforce the rights, no mere legal sanctions are going to make the system work.[43]

Of course, on Hare's view, to have a moral duty is simply to have internalized a firm disposition to behave in a certain way.

Some of the literature that is relevant to essay 6 does not consist in commentary on that essay. In an important paper, Philip Pettit discusses the special features of rights and argues that some forms of consequentialism can accommodate rights. Pettit argues that rights should be construed as "protective claims" that guarantee a person a certain sort of treatment. The consequentialist who restricts his deliberation accordingly can recognize rights and can be justified in doing so if able to identify a significant benefit that can be achieved only if one is not prepared to entertain trade-offs with other goods. Pettit suggests that "the dignity which is usually said to accrue to a right-holder . . . is an intuitively important benefit" that cannot be achieved unless those who

41. Greenawalt, "Utilitarian Justifications," p. 145.

42. R. M. Hare, "Utility and Rights: Comment on David Lyons's Essay," in *Ethics, Economics, and the Law,* ed. J. R. Pennock and J. W. Chapman (New York: New York University Press, 1982), p. 153.

43. Hare, "Utility and Rights," p. 154.

might interfere with one's self-governance make clear that they will not entertain the possibility of interference. On Pettit's view, then, consequentialism can be reconciled with rights if it ranks some goods (such as dignity) considerably higher than others (such as welfare).[44]

Several commentators have expressed reservations about the interpretation of Mill that is offered in my essays. Scholars generally prefer an act-utilitarian reading of Mill. This may be a reflection of the fact that consequentialists generally and utilitarians in particular tend to favor "act" versions of those theory-types.[45]

The scholarly literature on Mill has been greatly enriched in recent years by significant articles and book-length studies, the most notable being Fred Berger's treatise.[46] Some of those writings address the interpretive theses of the present volume.[47] Berger systematically discusses various revisionist readings proposed by my essays and related proposals by others.[48]

More recently, David Brink has taken the interpretive issues a long stride or two beyond the essays collected here. Brink argues persuasively that Mill endorses a *"deliberative* conception of happiness or welfare"*: "Happiness consists in large part in the exercise of those higher capacities that distinguish us from other animals, . . . especially our capacities for rational deliberation."[49] This renders some liberties considerably more important than others:

44. Philip Pettit, "The Consequentialist Can Recognise Rights," *Philosophical Quarterly* 38(1988): 42–53. The possibility of such an argument is suggested in the part of essay 6 entitled "Extension of the Argument."

45. I fear that the extensional equivalence argument of my *Forms and Limits of Utilitarianism* (Oxford: Clarendon, 1965) may have restored some of act-consequentialism's allure.

46. Fred R. Berger, *Happiness, Justice, and Freedom* (Berkeley: University of California Press, 1984). See the Bibliography for books by Donner, Gray, Ryan, and Ten and for an important series of articles by D. G. Brown.

47. See Fred R. Berger, "John Stuart Mill on Justice and Fairness"; David Copp, "The Iterated Utilitarianism of J. S. Mill"; D. P. Dryer, "Justice, Liberty, and the Principle of Utility in Mill"; and L. W. Sumner, "The Good and the Right"—all in *New Essays on John Stuart Mill and Utilitarianism* [special issue], ed. W. E. Cooper, K. Nielsen, and S. C. Patten, *Canadian Journal of Philosophy Suppl.* 5(1979): 63–136.

48. See Berger, *Happiness, Justice, and Freedon,* pp. 105–20 (on Mill's principle of utility), 214–25 (on imperfect duties), and 253–59 (on Mill's principle of liberty).

49. David O. Brink, "Mill's Deliberative Utilitarianism," *Philosophy and Public Affairs* 21(1992): 79.

Some liberties are necessary conditions to the realization of the dominant component in human welfare, namely, the exercise of rational capacities. For this reason the liberties that are essential to the exercise of rational capacities are themselves dominant (though not intrinsic) goods and have the status of rights; they trump or defeat claims that we could promote lesser goods (e.g., pleasure or preference satisfaction) by interfering with these liberties. Recognizing a right to these liberties, therefore, is the way to maximize value.[50]

Brink's reading of Mill plays a role in the interpretive literature parallel to Pettit's contributions to consequentialist theory. They give some reason to believe that utilitarianism might, after all, accommodate rights.

---

50. Brink, "Mill's Deliberative Utilitarianism," p. 92.

1

Rights, Claimants, and Beneficiaries

To have a right, Bentham held, is to be the *beneficiary* of another's duty or obligation.[1] This theory, one of the more attractive and plausible suggestions about the nature of rights, appears supported by innumerable cases. It is reflected in the notion common to laymen, lawyers, and philosophers that someone with a right is on the advantageous side of a legal or moral relation. It promises to explain why rights are such valuable and important commodities. And it seems bolstered by a variety of facts, for example, that compensation or reparation is often required, and might always be required, when one's rights are violated or infringed.

But Bentham's theory has been criticized, most notably by H.L.A. Hart, and it is not now, I think, very widely or seriously entertained.

Earlier versions of this essay were read at Cornell University and the Universities of Massachusetts, Michigan, Pittsburgh, Texas, and Waterloo, where I received helpful comments and criticisms. I also benefited greatly from discussions with Norman Malcolm and Michael Stocker and from the suggestions of Ellen Coleman, Robert Monk, William Nelson, and John Turner.

1. This is my formulation, not Bentham's; it encompasses the two interpretations of Bentham's theory discussed in this essay. Bentham's relevant views about rights are expressed in various ways in various writings; I shall give some references in the course of the notes. Others may be found in H.L.A. Hart, "Bentham: Lecture on a Master Mind," *British Academy Proceedings* 48(1962): 297–320 (hereafter "Bentham") and his *Essays on Bentham: Jurisprudence and Legal Theory* (Oxford: Clarendon, 1982). See also C. K. Ogden, ed., *Bentham's Theory of Fictions* (Patterson, N.J.: Littlefield, Adams, 1959).

Bentham's theory concerns what it is to have a right, not what a right is. For the notion that a right is an interest, see, e.g., John W. Salmond, *Salmond on Jurisprudence,* 11th ed., ed. G. Williams (London: Sweet & Maxwell, 1957), chap. 10.

This is unfortunate, since none of the received arguments appears decisive against the beneficiary theory as such. In this essay I shall attempt to show that Hart's objections are weaker than they must at first appear because their force is largely dispelled against but one form of beneficiary theory. Another, ''qualified'' beneficiary theory is much less vulnerable to Hart's objections and still worthy of our consideration.

In the first section I develop and explain the beneficiary theory and distinguish two versions that might be attributed to Bentham. In the second section I argue that being a beneficiary, in a certain qualified sense, is sufficient for having a right. In the third section I chiefly discuss some difficulties surrounding the claim that being a beneficiary is a necessary condition as well.

In this essay I shall assume that straightforward statements about moral rights can be analyzed in terms of moral obligations in the same way that statements about legal rights can be analyzed in terms of legal obligations. I shall take the beneficiary theory to apply to moral as well as legal rights.[2]

I

Many writers have held that the notion of a right must be analyzed in terms of duty or obligation—or, more generally, in terms of requirements or prohibitions on someone's behavior.[3] This is Bentham's view:

> It is by imposing obligations, or by abstaining from imposing them, that rights are established or granted. . . . How can a *right* of property in land be conferred on me? It is by imposing upon everybody else the obligation of not touching its productions, &c. &c. How can I possess the *right* of going into all the streets of a city? It is because there exists no obligation which hinders me, and because everybody is bound by an obligation not to hinder me.[4]

2. Bentham restricted his theory to legal rights. In attacking natural rights, he rejected rights that are not recognized and enforced but did so for reasons independent of his analysis of rights in terms of beneficial obligations; see essay 6.

3. The difference between duties or obligations, on the one hand, and mere prohibitions and requirements, on the other, will be touched on later. For the purposes of this essay differences between ''duty'' and ''obligation'' can be ignored.

4. Jeremy Bentham, ''A General View of a Complete Code of Laws,'' in *The Works of Jeremy Bentham,* ed. J. Bowring (hereafter *Works*), 3: 181, cf. 159. See also Jeremy Bentham, ''Pannomial Fragments,'' *Works,* 3: 217–22.

So the idea of obligation is central to that of a right, though these ideas may be related in different ways, according to the type of right in question. Property rights, as Bentham suggests, involve others' obligations to forbear from using the property without permission. Some rights imply others' obligations even more obviously, for example, a right to be paid ten dollars by Jones, a right to be cared for by one's parents, a right to be given equal consideration, a right not to be killed; and in such cases the statement of the right may be held to be equivalent to the statement of the corresponding obligation. But a right to *do* (or to refrain from doing) something has as its core the *absence* of an obligation to do otherwise.[5] Even here, however—as Bentham's second example and his general remarks suggest, and as others have agreed—one's right also seems to involve others' obligations, that is, obligations to refrain from interfering.

Bentham held, then, that rights can be "reduced" to duties or obligations. But he did not hold the closely associated view, that rights and duties are necessarily "correlatives." That is, he did not hold that duties always imply rights. This is important to Bentham's analysis of rights. To see why, let us consider the notion of correlativity briefly.

When Bernard owes Alvin ten dollars, we have equal reason to ascribe a right to Alvin (to be paid ten dollars by Bernard) and an obligation to Bernard (to pay Alvin ten dollars), and whatever would falsify one ascription would likewise falsify the other. Neither the right nor the obligation can arise without the other; and if one is discharged, waived, canceled, voided, forfeited, or otherwise extinguished, the other must be extinguished as well. For the ground of the obligation—the debt—is the title of the right. Alvin's right and Bernard's obligation *necessarily coexist;* one implies the other.

---

5. Or perhaps it has as its core a sphere of activity in which one is free to do as one pleases: the right to do X may include not only the absence of an obligation to refrain from doing X but also the absence of an obligation to do X. These rights concern what one may permissibly do. Rights that correlate with others' obligations concern what others must or must not do. These two kinds of rights are distinguished from what lawyers call "powers," which concern what one can do with legal or moral effect, and "immunities," which concern what others cannot do to one. See Wesley Newcomb Hohfeld, *Fundamental Legal Conceptions as Applied in Judicial Reasoning,* ed. W. W. Cook (New Haven: Yale University Press, 1964) and *Salmond on Jurisprudence,* chap. 10. Bentham does not apply his theory to powers and immunities, which may not amount to rights unless they, too, suitably involve interests. Being incapable of inheriting property constitutes an "immunity," but that hardly counts as a right. Hart suggests that a relation to individual choice unifies rights.

This pattern of correlations is extremely common. It obtains not only when debts are owed but also when certain other relations exist between two (or possibly more) particular individuals—as a consequence, for example, of promises and contracts, wrongful injuries that require reparation, good turns that require reciprocation, relationships such as parent to child and teacher to student. In such cases it is natural to speak of *A*'s having certain rights *against B* and of *B*'s having (or *owing*) corresponding obligations *to A*.[6] And it is important that, when obligations are so grounded on such special relations or transactions and consequently can be said to be "owed" to particular persons, we can infer that the person to whom the obligation is owed has a corresponding right and that he holds it against the person with the obligation.

It is important to note what these words will be taken to signify. When *A*, in particular, holds a certain right *against B*, *A* is a *claimant* against *B*. A "claimant" is one empowered to press or waive a claim against someone with a corresponding duty or obligation. He can, if he wishes, release the other from his obligation and cancel it, or he can insist upon its performance. A creditor, for example, is a claimant against his debtor. A promisee is a claimant against one who makes a valid and binding promise to him. So too is a person to whom a debt of reparation is owed because of wrongful injury done. A claimant is thus one to whom the performance of a duty or obligation is *owed*—he is the one who holds the claim against the other and who is entitled to administer the claim as he chooses. There are obviously moral as well as legal claimants in this sense.

The pattern of relations between rights and obligations I have just described does not seem to be universal. When behavior is simply required or prohibited by law or morals, without presupposing such special relations or transactions between particular individuals as I have mentioned, we often say that "duties" or "obligations" are imposed. But since these duties or obligations are *not* "owed" to anyone in particular, we cannot determine who, if anyone, has corresponding rights by noting to whom they are "owed." Indeed, although rights sometimes do correlate with such duties or obligations, we cannot infer *that there are* such rights merely from the fact *that there are* such duties or obligations. This point is essential to a theory like Bentham's.

6. See Joel Feinberg's very helpful discussion in "Duties, Rights, and Claims," *American Philosophical Quarterly* 3(1966): 137–42.

Consider the following contrast. When children who have reached their majority are required by law to support their aged and indigent parents it seems plausible to say that their parents have a legal right to such support from their children. But if children are required by law to inform the authorities of their parents' seditious remarks and activities (for which the punishment is death), we may have some hesitancy in saying that their parents have corresponding rights to be informed upon by their children. (We would be inclined to ascribe such rights only in very special circumstances.) From the fact that the law requires that *A* be treated in a certain way, it does not follow, without any further assumptions, that *A* may be said to have a right to be treated in that way. That is, rights do not follow from duties or obligations, or from requirements or prohibitions, alone. Other conditions must be satisfied.

Bentham held that rights are conferred only by beneficial obligations: "To assure to individuals the possession of a certain good, is to confer a *right* upon them."[7] Goods are assured by imposing duties or obligations, by requiring acts or forbearances of others. Obligations do not correspond to rights unless they protect or serve rather than harm or threaten those they directly concern. So Bentham held that rights "correlate" with duties or obligations in the following way, by virtue of the very notion of a right: rights imply duties, but only beneficial ones. And thus duties do not necessarily correspond to rights; they do so only when they "assure goods."

It will be useful to characterize Bentham's theory as follows: to have a right is, essentially, to be the *beneficiary* of another's duty or obligation (or of some requirement or prohibition upon another's behavior). But this needs certain qualifications before it can properly be evaluated.

A beneficiary in the relevant sense does not necessarily benefit from the existence of the corresponding obligation. First, benefits cannot be conferred by performance of an obligation if the obligation is not performed. Second, a beneficiary may ultimately lose, rather than gain, from performance of the obligation—but for irrelevant reasons. Alvin might spend on drink the ten dollars he receives from Bernard in payment of the debt, wreck his car, and suffer serious injury—none of which would happen if Bernard failed to discharge his debt. Third, the "service" required by an obligation, such as not robbing and not as-

7. Bentham, *Works*, 3: 159.

saulting, may be "negative," rather than "positive."[8] As Bentham uses the term, one may "benefit" in the sense of *not losing* rather than in the sense of gaining; what may be "assured" is not so much a good as the avoidance of an evil. The term "beneficiary" can be misleading, therefore, but we shall continue to use it with these implicit qualifications.

Beyond this point, Bentham's precise position is difficult to determine. Two main currents run through Bentham's discussions of rights, from which one can construct two significantly different versions of beneficiary theory.

The unqualified beneficiary theory. One the one hand Bentham seems to hold that rights are conferred whenever (and only when) rules that impose duties are justified according to the utilitarian test, that is when the rules and the duties they impose are useful.[9] Good laws serve the interests of individuals, and these laws confer rights. But bad laws impose duties from which no one (or hardly anyone) stands to benefit and therefore fail to confer rights. Various passages suggest that Bentham held the unqualified beneficiary theory, as attributed to him by Hart: that someone with a right is simply one "likely to benefit" or "capable of benefiting" or one who "stands to benefit" by the performance of a duty.[10]

This is the theory attacked by Hart. We shall examine his objections, but we need not share his alternative view in order to see that such a theory, straightforwardly understood, could not be correct. It is open to innumerable counterexamples. Suppose that Bernard owed Alvin ten dollars and also that Alvin has privately decided to give Charles a present if and only if the debt is repaid. Let us suppose further that Alvin is in no way indebted to Charles and that he has made no promises—not even tacit promises—to give Charles anything. It would seem then that Alvin has the right that corresponds to Bernard's obligation (the right to be paid ten dollars by Bernard) and that Charles has no relevant right (save the right to accept a gift from Alvin, which is clearly *independent* of Bernard's obligation). But the unqualified beneficiary theory does not differentiate between the positions of Alvin and Charles with respect to Bernard's obligation, and seems to imply that each has a right, since each stands to benefit from the performance of Bernard's obligation.

8. Bentham, *Works*, 3: 159, 181.

9. Bentham, *Works*, 3: 181, 220–21.

10. See Hart, "Bentham," pp. 313–15; and Hart, "Are There Any Natural Rights?" *Philosophical Review* 64(1955): 180–81.

(Indeed, Charles stands to benefit more than Alvin.) But Charles would not for that reason be said to have a right.

The qualified beneficiary theory. If the theory is to be rendered more plausible, the notion of a "beneficiary" must be refined. It seems clear that the performance of Bernard's obligation is relevant differently to Alvin's benefiting and Charles's benefiting, but the difference is elusive. Charles's benefiting is related contingently to Bernard's obligation, but the same is true of Alvin's benefiting: from the fact that Bernard pays Alvin ten dollars, it does not *follow* that Alvin benefits. And yet the connection between Bernard's performance and Alvin's benefiting does not seem *as* contingent as the connection between Bernard's performance and Charles's benefiting. How should the relevant relation be understood?

Some remarks by Bentham suggest that a person with a right is a "beneficiary" in the sense that he is *supposed* to benefit by or from the performance of another's obligation.[11] Alvin is the direct, intended beneficiary of Bernard's obligation; Charles is not.

This suggestion seems to fit situations in which we believe that we have obligations corresponding to others' rights. Our statement of what a given obligation requires need not refer to the conferring of benefits *as such:* like Bernard's obligation to pay Alvin the ten dollars he owes him, it may simply require a certain act, forbearance, or pattern of behavior. But we would fail to *understand* the obligations that we have—we would be unable to determine what we ought to do on the basis of them—unless we could also say whether or not those they directly concern are supposed to benefit from them. And it seems plausible to suggest that, when we fully understand the obligations we have that *do* correspond to others' *rights,* we also see that those they directly concern *are* supposed to benefit from them. This is patently true in some cases; obligations of indebtedness, reparation, and reciprocation, for example, essentially involve and require the returning or restoring of goods to particular persons. Other cases are more difficult, particularly obligations imposed by the criminal law and analogous rules of morality, on the one hand, and promissory or contractual obligations on the other. I shall deal with these separately and in some detail.

According to the qualified beneficiary theory, then, a person with a right is not one who merely stands to benefit from the performance of

11. See, e.g., Bentham, *Works,* 3: 159.

another's obligation. He is one for whom a good is "assured," or an evil obstructed, by requirements or prohibitions upon others' behavior, in the sense that some other person or persons are required to act or forbear in ways designed or intended to serve, secure, promote, or protect his interests or an interest of his. He is a beneficiary in what I shall call the "qualified" sense of the term; he is "the party to be benefited."[12] According to the qualified beneficiary theory, such persons and only such persons have rights.

II

Hart maintains, against Bentham, that

> According to the strict usage of most modern English jurists following Austin . . . the person who has a right is something more than a possible beneficiary of duty; he is the person who may, at his option, demand the execution of the duty or waive it . . . and it is neither neccessary nor sufficient (though it is usually true) that he will also benefit from the performance of it.[13]

In this section I shall argue, with regard to Hart's criminal law examples, that the qualified beneficiary theory gives a sufficient condition for having a right (although the unqualified theory fails to do so). In the next section I extend the argument to promissory rights and discuss Hart's claim that the theory fails to provide a necessary condition as well.

Hart agrees with Bentham that rights imply duties or obligations but that the latter do not always imply the former. But Hart's reasons for saying that not all duties imply rights are different from Bentham's. Bentham, as we have seen, holds that the law can and unfortunately often does impose "barren" duties or "ascetic" obligations, that is, duties or obligations without beneficiaries, which have no corresponding rights. But Hart holds that duties without claimants have no corresponding rights. And these positions are different because being a claimant is not a necessary condition for being a beneficiary of another's duty. This

12. So Bentham defines "beneficiary" in his discussion of trusts (*Works*, 1: 106), though he does not argue that beneficiaries (and only such persons) have rights in the relevant sense.

13. Hart, "Bentham," p. 315. For other criticisms, see Hart, *Definition and Theory in Jurisprudence* (Oxford: Clarendon, 1953).

is shown by the fact that there are obligations with beneficiaries but without private claimants in the sense discussed above. Under the civil (as distinct from the criminal) law, private individuals administer their own rights; they alone can initiate proceedings against others who violate or threaten their rights. But there are no such private claimants under the criminal law—only *complainants*. For the substantive rules of the criminal law impose duties or obligations that cannot be canceled by a private party; they can be ''canceled'' only by a change in the rules. A private individual, such as the victim of a criminal offense, can impede or aid a prosecution, but he lacks the analogous legal ''power'' his counterpart has under the civil law to sue. Public officials have both the legal power and the responsibility of enforcing the criminal law. Many civil law obligations arise from special relations or transactions between the parties,[14] whereby such obligations are incurred or assumed, but criminal law obligations are simply laid down or imposed and thus it is less natural to speak of them as being ''owed'' to particular individuals, and they are not ''owed'' in the full sense discussed above.

A similar distinction can be drawn within the class of moral duties and obligations. Some can be incurred or assumed (e.g., by promising), and these can be canceled by the one to whom the promise is made and to whom its performance is owed. But some moral principles simply forbid or require, they lay down what one may not or must do; and while these may be said to impose ''duties'' or ''obligations,'' they cannot always be waived or canceled.

Accordingly, Hart claims that, strictly speaking, there are no rights under the criminal law or in the analogous part of morality, because such duties or obligations are not administered by private claimants. Hart observes that jurists generally prefer not to speak of ''rights'' under the criminal law, for reasons akin to his. But he *also* concedes that usage differs on this point:

> A somewhat wider usage of the expression ''a right'' is common among non-lawyers and especially among writers on political theory who might not hesitate to say, for example, that when the *criminal* law forbids murder and assault it thereby secures to individuals a right to security of

14. This point has been revised in light of Hart, ''Bentham on Legal Rights,'' in *Oxford Essays in Jurisprudence: Second Series,* ed. A.W.B. Simpson, pp. 171–201 (Oxford: Clarendon, 1973)—which further develops Hart's account of rights.

the person, even though he is in no position to waive a duty imposed by the criminal law.[15]

The so-called "wider" usage lacks the requirement that the person with the right (or anyone else) be a claimant. Hart goes on to suggest that such a wider use of "right" can be tolerated if it retains a central feature of the allegedly strict sense explicated by his claimant theory. We might continue to speak of rights under the criminal law provided we recognize that laws which confer rights as well as impose duties "also provide, in a distinctively distributive way, for the individual who has the right." Hart's position seems to be this. When the term "right" is used strictly, a person with a right has *his own* special powers as a claimant, his "limited sovereignty over the person who has the duty." Under a tolerable wider use, a distributive feature would be retained when talk of rights under the criminal law is confined to cases in which the law protects the security *of the individual*—as opposed to, say, the security of the community as a whole—that is, where a breach of such a duty "necessarily involves the infliction of harm upon a specific or (in Bentham's language) 'assignable' individual." But Hart claims that Bentham's analysis contains no such distributive feature, because on Bentham's theory one can qualify as having a right if he is merely "a member of a class who as a class may be indiscriminately benefited by the performance of a duty." For Bentham's theory would allegedly accord rights not only to persons protected by rules such as those forbidding murder and assault—who might be said to have "rights" under a tolerably extended usage of the term—but also to those who *might possibly* benefit by the performance of *any* useful duties, even though they do not serve the interests of individuals directly. The breach of such legal duties as income tax and military service (Hart's examples) does not necessarily involve the infliction of harm upon a specific individual, "but at the most merely makes it likely that the community as a whole will be less secure."[16]

As Hart says, certain *ascriptions* of rights (e.g., under the criminal law) are "wider" than others (e.g., under the civil law) in the sense that the former lack implications which the latter have that the person with the right is a claimant. For rights under the civil law, unlike rights under the criminal law, may be ascribed as rights "against" those having the

15. Hart, "Bentham," p. 315.
16. Hart, "Bentham," p. 315.

corresponding duties, which are reciprocally "owed." (Similar remarks apply to classes of moral rights and their ascriptions.) But from this it does not follow that ascribing rights where there are no claimants involves a wider *sense of the term* "right" or uses an extended concept. The differences between the ascriptions *as a whole* might be explained by the fact that some are qualified as rights "against" particular persons while others are not, depending on the sorts of conditions that warrant the ascription of the right. Unless we assume that being a claimant is essential to having a right in the "strict" sense of the term, we have as yet no reason to suppose that the concept of a right itself is extended when it happens not to be instantiated as a right "against" another.

Straightforward talk about rights is not generally confined to contexts in which there are private claimants. Rights may be ascribed, for example, in the context of the criminal law for the purpose of noting that some act or omission is not unlawful, when one is challenged, when interference is threatened, or to draw certain contrasts. For example, a motorist has a right to make a right turn on a red light in some jurisdictions which he lacks in others because of differences between the respective traffic laws. Such a right is not held against or with respect to any particular person, but this does not seem to make it any less of a right or a right in only an extended or loose sense of the term.

A right not to be killed may be analogous. Is it clear that we speak loosely or that we stretch our ordinary notion of a right when we ascribe, in the context of the criminal law or on the basis of general moral prohibitions, the right not to be killed? One way of finding out is by determining whether there is a single acceptable account of rights within both sorts of context, that is, with and without private claimants. This is what the beneficiary theory purports to give.

Now let us consider more directly the force of Hart's objection against the beneficiary theory concerning rights without claimants under the criminal law. Hart maintains that rules such as those forbidding murder and assault may be said to confer rights, as the beneficiary theory implies, but only in a wider sense of the term; while rules requiring payment of income tax and military service, even when useful, cannot be said to confer rights, even in such a wider sense, although the beneficiary theory implies they do. Hart says that rights can be ascribed in the former cases because such a usage retains a certain "distributive" feature of the notion of a right, since the breach of such a duty "necessarily involves the infliction of harm upon a specific . . . individual."

The qualified beneficiary theory distinguishes these cases, too. It accounts for those in which (as Hart agrees) rights can be ascribed, but it does not regard the ascriptions as involving a wider sense of the term. Rights are ascribed to those whose interests are to be served by the prohibitions. The theory does not imply that every useful duty has a corresponding right. Hart's objection is directed against the unqualified beneficiary theory and, as I shall try to show, it has no force against the qualified theory.

There is another and I think more obvious and plausible way of understanding why rights are and can be ascribed when murder and assault are prohibited. Such rules "assure goods" or obstruct evils to those they are supposed to protect. The qualified beneficiary theory can account for such rights without implying that every useful duty has a corresponding right.

Any rule that has a utilitarian justification and is in that sense "useful" ultimately serves (or can reasonably be expected to serve) the interest of individuals, but rules can do so in different ways. The rules that serve individuals most directly do so by imposing *beneficial* duties, in a qualified sense, which implies that there are beneficiaries in the sense employed by the qualified beneficiary theory. Rules such as those forbidding murder and assault are of this type; they can only be understood as requiring that we not harm or injure others in certain ways. The duties they impose require treating others in ways that are meant to serve certain of their interests. The rules define the classes of persons protected, and any member of such a class is a beneficiary in the qualified sense. He does not merely "stand to benefit" by the performance of such a duty, nor does he merely stand to suffer if the duty is breached. From the point of view of the rules and the duties they impose, such a person is neither a lucky bystander in one case nor an unlucky one in the other. He is one who, according to the rules, is not to be harmed in such a way. His loss at the hands of the person with the duty would be directly relevant to the question whether the duty is breached. Despite the fact that such a person cannot be said to have a right "against" anyone in particular—since he cannot waive or cancel the corresponding obligation and it does not rest upon any *special* relation between him and those bound by the rules—and despite the fact that the duty is not "owed" to him in particular, it does seem plausible to say that he is *entitled* to be treated in a certain way (e.g., not to be assaulted or killed) and that saying this is not speaking loosely. For others are duty-bound so to treat him, and his *right* does correspond to and correlate with their duties.

Other rules that can be justified on utilitarian grounds serve individuals much less directly. If there is a good utilitarian reason for requiring payment of income tax, for example, benefits to individuals must be expected ultimately to accrue. But the possible, intended, or desired benefits that might ultimately accrue to individuals do not flow directly from the performance of such duties, and no harm results directly, if at all, from their breach. Duties imposed by such rules I shall call (merely) "useful." Such duties have no beneficiaries in the qualified sense. Money collected from income tax payments can be used to serve the community, and therefore its members, in various ways. But these ways are not determined by the act of payment itself. Most important, the content of the duty to pay income tax concerns payment and payment only. It does not concern the uses to which the revenue might be put. One who might possibly benefit from the use of such revenues, and accordingly may stand to benefit from the performance of the duty to pay income tax, is not a beneficiary in the qualified sense. His benefit or loss is not directly relevant to the question whether or not the duty is discharged.

There is not even a traceable connection, normally, between someone's gain or loss and another person's discharge or breach of his duty to pay income tax. The payment marks the beginning of a long, complex chain that may, but does not necessarily, lead to benefits to individuals. Generally speaking, a particular person's payment or nonpayment is neither necessary nor sufficient for bringing about or preventing another person's ultimate benefits or losses. Usually, benefits cannot accrue in the long run unless observance of such duties is widespread. Even if it is widespread, the actual result depends on how the money is used. Even when individuals do receive benefits that are partly traceable to income tax revenues, it remains extremely unlikely, if not impossible, that we should be able to ascribe anyone's benefits to particular performances of the duty to pay income tax. If harm results or benefits do not accrue because payments are commonly withheld, it is again extremely unlikely, if not impossible, that particular losses could be ascribed to particular breaches. Moreover, no loss will be caused by nonpayment unless breaches are common. So it is neither necessarily the case nor even likely that anyone will suffer or lose as a consequence of one breach (or several breaches) of a merely useful duty.

Hart's objection is, then, that the unqualified beneficiary theory implies that merely useful as well as beneficial duties give rise to rights. This is because such a weak condition as "Someone stands to benefit by the performance of another's duty" *must* be satisfied whenever useful duties are imposed. But this objection has no force against the qualified beneficiary theory, since merely useful duties have no beneficiaries in the qualified sense. So, while it may be implausible to say that a merely useful duty gives rise to a corresponding right, it is also difficult to construe the qualified beneficiary theory as implying it. Hart's objection has been met. Rights correspond to obligations under the criminal law in just the way Hart claims, according to the qualifed beneficiary theory. Rights correlate with beneficial duties and not with merely useful ones.

Before closing this section it is worth noting that the qualified beneficiary theory accounts for rights that are related, indirectly, to such duties as military service and payment of income tax. Consider, for example, those persons who *qualify by law* as recipients of governmental services and expenditures (e.g., public education, unemployment compensation, garbage collection). The rules that govern such expenditures also provide criteria for qualification. One who qualifies by law would seem legally *entitled* to the benefits or services and thus to have a legal right to them. These rights can readily be accounted for by the qualified beneficiary theory. For *corresponding* duties—not duties to pay income tax, but duties to distribute the benefits and administer the services—fall upon those whose job it is to do such things. So, the qualified beneficiary theory seems also to account for rights that Hart does not consider. And it does so by using one purported sense of "right," which is applied in other contexts as well.[17]

III

Hart's more formidable objection to the beneficiary theory concerns the case of the "third-party beneficiary."[18] Promises—when they are valid

17. Hart's claimant or choice theory can account for rights where provision of benefits is conditional upon application, but it cannot accommodate cases in which there is no choice or option to exercise, e.g., where free public education is also compulsory.

18. See Hart, "Bentham," p. 314, and "Are There Any Natural Rights?" pp. 180ff.

and binding—engender rights to promisees and obligations to promisors. A promisee often stands to benefit from the promised performance, but when a promise is meant to benefit a "third party" (i.e., one who is not a party to the agreement), then, according to Hart, the promisee, as usual, acquires a right even though he is not a beneficiary, while the third party, who is supposed to benefit, acquires no right. This shows that being a beneficiary is neither necessary nor sufficient for having a right.

In Hart's example, a son extracts a promise from another (let us say a friend) to care for his aged mother in his absence. Hart argues that the son has the right. The promise is made *to* him and he, therefore, has the claim against the friend. The friend's performance is *owed* to or *due* him. He alone can press or waive the claim, can insist upon its performance or release his friend from the promise. If the promise is not kept, Hart argues, the son is *wronged* even if he is not harmed. But the mother (a third-party beneficiary) has no right. She might be harmed if the promise is not kept, but she cannot be wronged. For the promise is not made *to her,* and thus the performance is not owed to or due her. One with a right admittedly may be, and usually is, a beneficiary of a duty. But this is not what it is to have a right. The promisee alone has a moral claim upon the promisor. He is

> morally in a position to determine by his choice how [the promisor] shall act and in this way to limit [the promisor's] freedom of choice; and it is this fact, not the fact that he stands to benefit, that makes it appropriate to say that he has *a right*.[19]

I shall try to show the limits of this objection to the qualified beneficiary theory. First, I shall argue that Hart's objection rests in part upon a misconstrual of the third-party beneficiary's position with respect to another's obligation. Because Hart considers only the unqualified beneficiary theory with its inadequate notion of a beneficiary, he assimilates the mother's position in his example to that of persons who merely "stand to benefit" by the performance of a duty and have no relevant rights. The alternative suggestion, offered by the qualified beneficiary theory, is that the mother, like those in other contexts who may properly be said to have rights although they are not claimants, can be accorded a right precisely because she is a beneficiary in the qualified sense. Then I

19. Hart, "Are There Any Natural Rights?" p. 180.

shall examine the question whether claimants, who seem clearly to have rights, are necessarily beneficiaries—in other words, whether being a beneficiary is a necessary condition for having a right.

Hart concedes that "common usage" may sanction the ascription of rights to beneficiaries—to animals and infants, for example, who are said to have rights to proper treatment because we have duties not to ill-treat them. But Hart maintains that this way of speaking employs only "the philosopher's generalized sense of 'duty'" and that it makes "an idle use of the expression 'a right.'" He contends that "the moral situation can be simply and adequately described here by saying that it is wrong or that we ought not to ill-treat" babies or animals. But "right" and "duty" have a "specific force" in other contexts that cannot be captured by such uses of "wrong" and "ought."[20] When "right" and "duty" are used strictly, and not merely in a "generalized" sense, the person with the duty may be said to be "bound to" the person with the right. The right-holder is a claimant, who controls the duty. Thus the friend has a duty "to" the son, to whom he *owes* the promised performance. But the friend has a duty "to" the mother only in the sense that his duty concerns her. The friend does not "owe" the performance to the mother, and thus she has no right to the promised services, for she has no right "against" the friend.

Hart draws our attention to special features of our discourse about rights that set it off from talk about what ought to be done or what it would be wrong to do or about "duties" that are not "owed" to claimants. He suggests that the beneficiary theory obscures the differences between these sectors of moral and legal discourse. Hart's view involves a threefold distinction, between (a) contexts in which rights in the "strict" sense can be ascribed; (b) contexts in which rights can be ascribed only in a wider sense; and (c) contexts in which "duties" may be ascribed, but not rights. The qualified beneficiary theory makes similar distinctions but draws the lines somewhat differently. Corresponding to Hart's contexts (a) and (b) are those in which ascriptions of rights can be made in a single sense of the term, although the ascriptions are warranted by different sorts of conditions (depending on whether or not the duty or obligation is "owed" to the person with the right). Corre-

---

20. Hart, "Are There Any Natural Rights?" p. 181. See also Hart, "Legal and Moral Obligation," in *Essays in Moral Philosophy,* ed. A. I. Melden (Seattle: University of Washington Press, 1958), esp. pp. 82–84, 100–105.

sponding to Hart's context (c) is that in which duties or obligations are not beneficial and rights cannot be ascribed, even if the duties are useful. Since such distinctions are not obscured by the qualified beneficiary theory, we need not dwell upon them.

We may consider instead what may be *common* to the various plausible ascriptions of rights to see whether being a beneficiary is both common and essential. Hart seems to suggest here that what is common when rights are ascribed in both the strict and the wider sense of the term is that the behavior of others that is required or prohibited *concerns* the person with the right. But this condition is surely not peculiar to requirements that might be held to correspond to rights. For as we have noted, Green's duty as executioner concerns the condemned Brown, while it is doubtful that Brown acquires a corresponding right. And it concerns Brown differently than the restrictions regarding babies and animals concern them. For our duties regarding babies and animals assure goods or obstruct evils to them.

The cases of babies and animals raise complications we need not examine here, for example, whether legal or moral personality or agency is required for the possession of rights. But it should be observed, nonetheless, that the position of the third-party beneficiary in Hart's example is different from that of babies and animals. The friend's obligation to serve the mother is not merely an instance of a general duty to refrain from harming the helpless. The friend's obligation arises from a specific agreement, and it is one he otherwise would not have. He has agreed to care for the mother. The mother is the one the promised services are intended to benefit. She is a direct, intended beneficiary.

Joel Feinberg suggests that Hart has overstated his point. Third-party beneficiaries are *sometimes* accorded rights in both morals and law. But, he says:

> it does not *follow necessarily* from the fact that a person is an intended beneficiary of a promised service that he has a right to it; whereas it always follows necessarily from the fact that a person is a promisee that he has a right to what is promised.[21]

Third-party beneficiaries can have rights, but "only in virtue of moral or judicial policies and rules." A third-party beneficiary's right seems to

21. Joel Feinberg, "Duties, Rights, and Claims," *American Philosophical Quarterly* 3(1966): 138.

follow from his position as beneficiary only when, for example, it is also plausible "to say that the promisor made a *tacit promise* to the beneficiary in addition to the express promise to his promisee." The parties to the agreement let the beneficiary know of it and he thereupon "acts in reliance on its performance."[22]

Here again, however, there is evidence that the objection hinges on a misconstrual of the mother's position. Feinberg's unwillingness to allow that third-party beneficiaries *necessarily* have rights seems based on the weak sense he and Hart attach to "third-party beneficiary." When this expression is so used that it can apply even to those who, as he says, merely "stand to gain, if only indirectly" or "who will profit in merely picayune and remote ways" from the promised performance,[23] a third-party beneficiary does *not* necessarily have a right. But if it is used in the qualified sense, the expression better characterizes the mother in Hart's example and it seems to *follow* that she has a right. The mother's interest is directly relevant to the friend's obligation. A complete specification of the friend's obligation includes *essential* reference to the mother, who is supposed to benefit by its performance. Her loss in case the promise is broken would not be a remote, accidental consequence of the friend's behavior; it would be the predictable and relevant consequence of a dereliction. The fact that she was not cared for would be the chief ground for saying that the friend had failed to discharge his obligation. Her receipt of the services would be the chief reason for saying that he had discharged his obligation. The friend's obligation is beneficial, and the mother is the beneficiary. The mother is *entitled* to the services required by the friend's obligation as one entitled to be treated in a certain way when another has an obligation specifically so to behave. Does she not *have a right* to be cared for by him?

Of course, in such a case, the mother may not be aware of the friend's promise and thus may not know that she is entitled to his services. But knowledge of the relevant facts is not a necessary condition for having a right. If ignorant of the agreement, she would be in no position to complain in case the friend broke his promise. But if she became aware of the relevant facts, she could legitimately complain and "press" her right (whether or not she was *further* inconvenienced because she relied upon the friend's help). Indeed, she might also refuse the services and

22. Feinberg, "Duties, Rights, and Claims," p. 138.
23. Feinberg, "Duties, Rights, and Claims," p. 137; see also p. 138 and n. 3.

thus effectively "release" the friend from his obligation, especially if she could care for herself and did not need the help arranged for her by her son. But this does not mean that she has a right *because* she is a *claimant;* it means, rather, that she *may act as* a claimant (if she is in a position to do so) precisely *because she has a right* to be cared for by the friend.

These considerations suggest once more that being a beneficiary is sufficient for having a right. But they do not show that being a beneficiary is a necessary condition, and thus the more serious threat posed by Hart's objection has not been met. For the son, as promisee, would seem to have a right against the friend. But the son does not appear to be a *beneficiary* in any straightforward sense. The promise is meant to benefit the mother, not the son, and she alone will benefit directly from the friend's care. Moreover, it is the friend's treatment of the mother, not his treatment of the son, that is relevant to the obligation, that determines whether or not it is discharged. This seems to indicate that being a beneficiary of a beneficial obligation is not a necessary condition of having a right.

If this part of Hart's objection is allowed, a defender of the beneficiary theory might be content with the following observations. The argument has tended to show that being a beneficiary of a beneficial obligation is, first of all, a sufficient condition for having a right. Hart's objection shows at best that being a beneficiary is not a necessary condition for having a right. But is does not show that rights are conferred even when there are no such beneficiaries. And this may not be an insignificant point. For outside the contexts of promises (contracts, agreements) counterexamples to the qualified beneficiary theory are not easy to find. In other contexts in both law and morals, it would seem that rights are ascribed when and only when obligations or restrictions upon others' behavior assure goods or obstruct evils to individuals and thus when breaches of the corresponding obligations would involve loss or harm to those with the rights. The apparent possibility of counterexamples arises because it does not seem to be a condition of a valid and binding promise that its performance serve the interests of the *promisee*. But in such cases there is at least a *third-party* beneficiary. It is difficult to imagine promises—or, generally, obligations that correspond to rights—which are valid and binding and yet serve no one's interests. On the contrary, our understanding of the nature of binding promises is shown by the fact that, when their fulfillment threatens unexpected disadvantages to those they are meant to serve, it would be wrong to keep them.

But if we pursue this line of argument and attempt to clarify the respects in which promises may be said to "serve someone's interests," then it would also appear that a promisee, even in a third-party beneficiary case, is a "beneficiary" in the qualified sense.

Suppose that Jones extracts a promise from Brown. The promise is not intended to benefit a third party, and there is no one who could plausibly be regarded as a "third-party beneficiary" in the appropriate sense. Brown makes the promise because he is led by Jones to believe that he, Jones, wants the promised act performed. But suppose that Jones is, in fact, unconcerned whether or not the promise is kept. He extracts the promise on the merest whim or out of malice. It seems clear that the conditions of a valid and binding promise are not satisfied (whether or not Brown knows this), and thus that Jones does not acquire *a right* to what was promised and that Brown incurs no *obligation* (although he may *think* that he is obligated). But if Jones had really wanted what was promised and Brown had freely agreed to do it, then— barring immoral purposes—a valid and binding promise would have been made.

One of the conditions of a valid and binding promise, and thus a condition of a right accruing to the promisee, is that he really wants what is promised.[24] Now this does not imply that there must be *benefits* in any straightforward sense. But it does, I think, imply that the obligation "assures a good" to the promisee. For it is the promisee's very want, wish, or desire *to have what is promised done* that the promise is *meant* to satisfy. And it is not implausible to suggest that the satisfaction of someone's (morally permissible) want, wish, or desire amounts to the conferring on him of a certain good.

If we try to imagine cases in which this claim is not satisfied, we shall find the ascription of a right and of a corresponding promissory obligation moot. Suppose, for example, that the promisee asks another to do him an injury or to kill him. We can imagine cases where, to avoid greater evil or unbearable pain, for example, such a promise might be reasonably requested and made and consequently binding. But in such cases there is also as much reason to say that the promise "assures a

24. See Jerome Schneewind, "A Note on Promising," *Philosophical Studies* 17(1966): 33–35.

certain good'' to the promisee. If there is no such good reason for the promise but only, say, a desire for self-destruction or mutilation, it is not at all clear that one would be morally free to make such a promise or that once made, the promise could be regarded as morally binding.

Let us return now to Hart's example. If a son extracts a promise from his friend to care for his aged mother in his absence, we might reasonably suppose that he does so because, say, he is concerned, as an affectionate son, about his mother's well-being; or, perhaps, because he thinks he is serving his own interests in providing for her care; or even because he wants to discharge what is to him a totally disagreeable filial obligation. We might reasonably suppose that the son really wants his mother cared for in his absence, that he has *some* interest in her being cared for, and that he extracts the promise accordingly. But let us not assume any such thing. Let us suppose instead that the son merely wants his friend to make such a promise, but that it is not part of his intention to provide for her care and that he has no interest in doing so.

Now, on the one hand, it might transpire that the friend acquires an obligation to care for the mother and that the mother acquires a right to the promised services—that the promise is binding to this degree, despite the son's secret indifference. For the mother has an interest that needs to be served and the friend freely agrees to serve it. But on the other hand, it would not seem that the son is truly entitled to complain if the friend fails to keep his promise. And that is because he has not satisfied the conditions necessary for acquiring such a right. If there is an obligation, it is not owed to the son (whether or not the friend knows it). If there is a legitimate claim, it is not the son's claim but the mother's; and if there is a right, it is not his but hers.

If there is such a difference between the son's moral status in this case and in Hart's original example, so that it is more plausible to ascribe a right to him in the latter than in the former, that difference has to do with the son's reasons for and his sincerity in extracting the promise. What is true of Hart's example that is not true here? The son wants his mother cared for, and for that reason asks his friend to do so. The reason he gives his friend is the same in both cases; but only in Hart's example is that really his reason. So in both cases at least part of the point of the promise is to satisfy such a desire or wish on the part of the son—to provide for his mother's care—but only in Hart's case will the keeping of the promise actually satisfy such a wish or desire.

This is not to say that the difference between the two cases, which may account for the fact that the son acquires a right in one but not the other, is the fact that in one but not the other the son stands to *benefit* from the promised performance. Nevertheless, the fact that the son has an interest in his mother's care and wants her cared for, coupled with the fact that it is *this* wish or desire of the son's that the friend's promise is designed to satisfy, shows that the friend's obligation ''assures a good'' to the son.

I do not mean to claim that this defense of the beneficiary theory is conclusive. I hope to have shown, rather, that the theory cannot be *dismissed* without further consideration. It is less vulnerable than its critics have supposed, largely because of the differences between its qualified and unqualified versions.

I shall conclude by considering an example that may indicate serious difficulties for the beneficiary theory. The example is suggested (in another connection) by Hart, who maintains that a certain class of moral rights correlates with ''political obligations''—obligations to conform to certain social rules. These rights and obligations arise, Hart says, in the following circumstances:

> When a number of persons conduct any joint enterprise according to rules and thus restrict their liberty, those who have submitted to these restrictions when required have a right to a similar submission from those who have benefited by their submission. The rules may provide that officials should have authority to enforce obedience and make further rules, and this will create a structure of legal rights and duties, but the moral obligation to obey the rules in such circumstances is due to the co-operating members of the society, and they have the correlative moral rights to obedience.[25]

As I have argued elsewhere,[26] certain qualifications should be added, at least to make the character of the present argument clear. These include (a) actual conformity to the rules is sufficiently widespread to produce some shareable good or to prevent some common evil; (b) this desirable result could not be achieved without such cooperation; (c) the benefits and burdens are fairly distributed; (d) the total benefits outweigh the burdens imposed; (e) *universal* cooperation by those who stand to benefit is *not* required to achieve the desirable end. The last condition is most important, because it explains how it is possible for a ''freeloader'' to

25. Hart, ''Are There Any Natural Rights?'' p. 185.
26. Lyons, *Forms and Limits of Utilitarianism,* chap. 5, sec. A.

take advantage of others' cooperation without performing as the rules require. The conditions also show that the duties imposed by the rules and the moral obligations to conform to them are not beneficial in the qualified sense employed above. For a single breach of such a rule is not sufficient for anyone's loss, and the performances required by these duties and obligations do not consist in directly serving the interests of someone with a correlative right.

The legal rule requiring payment of income tax might satisfy such conditions. If the conditions are satisfied, then, according to the argument given, one has a moral obligation to conform to the rule and others have a right to one's conformity or cooperation. The qualified beneficiary theory cannot account for such rights, since the legal duties in question are merely useful and the same holds for the moral obligation to obey such a law.

What are the connections between goods and rights in this case? On the one hand, there cannot be such an obligation unless the law, or system of law, is useful (as conditions (a), (b), and (d) require) and everyone stands to benefit (as condition (c) would I think require). So goods *are* essentially involved; but they are involved indirectly, as in the case of merely useful duties. For (as condition (e) seems to guarantee) the obligation to obey the law is *not* contingent on universal obedience being needed for the usefulness of the general practice. The idea that underlies such an obligation and its correlative right is that it would be *unfair* or *unjust* for someone who benefits from others' burdensome cooperation or conformity to fail to perform when his turn came. The idea is not that his failure to conform or cooperate would detract from the usefulness of the general practice or would decrease in any way the benefits that accrue to individuals. For according to the conditions of the argument, even the secret and harmless breaking of necessary rationing restrictions would be wrong and would involve the violation of such a right and the breach of such an obligation.

If this is correct, then it would seem that the only good that can be assured by such an obligation to obey the law in *each* of its instances is the *abstract* or *impersonal* good of justice. It is not a personal good, not a good *to* or *for* a person with a corresponding right. And this does not satisfy the conditions of the qualified beneficiary theory.

Utilitarians would, of course, deny that there is such an obligation, or would insist that it rests on the fact that nonconformity or noncoopera- tion can reasonably be expected to have bad results, by setting a bad example which may lead others to disobey, thus tending eventually to decrease the usefulness of the law. This suggests that the good assured to individuals is simply the confidence that their burdensome cooperation will not be in vain. Alternatively, utilitarians may seek to argue that the abstract or impersonal good of justice reduces, ultimately, to personal goods.

2

Mill's Theory of Morality

Many have assumed that utilitarianism requires one always to "maximize utility," regarding any other way of acting as wrong. This "act-utilitarian" doctrine has been criticized for imagining duties where none exist while ignoring special obligations that we bear towards other persons. In recent years, however, "rule-utilitarian" theories have said we should judge acts by reference to useful rules, which might account for special obligations and not require one to maximize utility. These developments have influenced our understanding of the classical utilitarians. J. O. Urmson, for example, reminds us that moral rules and obligations play a prominent role in Mill's *Utilitarianism*. But his rule-utilitarian reading of Mill has not gained wide acceptance, for the evidence he cites seems inconclusive and balanced by further considerations.[1]

I am grateful to Frederick Ellett, Ed Lewis, Stephen Massey, Gerald Postema, James Shayman, and Gail Wallace for their helpful comments on the ideas developed in this essay.

1. J. O. Urmson, "The Interpretation of the Moral Philosophy of J. S. Mill," *Philosophical Quarterly* 3(1953): 33–39. See also D. G. Brown, "Mill's Act-Utilitarianism," *Philosophical Quarterly* 24(1974): 67–68; Brian Cupples, "A Defense of the Received Interpretation of J. S. Mill," *Australasian Journal of Philosophy* 50(1972): 131–37; J. D. Mabbott, "Interpretations of Mill's *Utilitarianism*," *Philosophical Quarterly* 6(1956): 115–20; Maurice Mandelbaum, "Two Moot Issues in Mill's *Utilitarianism*," in *Mill*, ed. J. B. Schneewind (Garden City, N.Y.: Doubleday, 1968), pp. 206–33, esp. 207–21; Anthony Quinton, *Utilitarian Ethics* (London: Macmillan, 1973), chap. 3; Ernest Sosa, "Mill's *Utilitarianism*," in *Mill's Utilitarianism*, ed. James M. Smith and Ernest Sosa (Belmont, Calif.: Wadsworth, 1969): pp. 154–72, esp. 157–61. Cf. D. P. Dryer, "Mill's Utilitarianism," in *Essays on Ethics, Religion, and Society*, ed. J. M. Robson, The Collected Works of John Stuart Mill (Toronto: University of Toronto Press), 10: xcv–cxiii; and Alan Ryan, *The Philosophy of John Stuart Mill* (London: Macmillan, 1970), esp. chap. 12.

I do not expect this essay to settle, once and for all, the interpretation of Mill's utilitarianism. But it rests upon a passage that is clearly meant to be definitive, and therefore one on which considerable weight must be placed. The passage may help us better understand Bentham's influence on Mill. It suggests a utilitarianism more concerned with ends than with specific means (such as acts and social rules) of achieving those ends. This essay also lays the groundwork for an examination of Mill's distinctive theory of justice.

I. Morality and Expediency

In the last chapter of *Utilitarianism,* "On the Connection between Justice and Utility," Mill first looks at uses of the words "just" and "unjust" in order to identify the grounds for such appraisals. His examples show that not all questions of justice arise within or otherwise concern the law, and he argues that law cannot be the measure of justice because laws can be regarded as unjust. He indicates that the "moral" rules, obligations, and rights with which he is concerned are independent of both law and merely conventional morality.

But Mill believes there is an intimate connection between justice and law, through the notion that punishment and coercion would be fitting ways of dealing with injustice. These words are used quite broadly here, to cover "public disapprobation" as well as "legal constraint." This is where paragraph 14 begins:

> The above is, I think, a true account, as far as it goes, of the origin and progressive growth of the idea of justice. But we must observe, that it contains, as yet, nothing to distinguish that obligation from moral obligation in general. For the truth is, that the idea of penal sanction, which is the essence of law, enters not only into the conception of injustice, but into that of any kind of wrong. We do not call anything wrong, unless we mean to imply that a person ought to be punished in some way or other for doing it; if not by law, by the opinion of his fellow creatures; if not by opinion, by the reproaches of his own conscience. This seems the real turning point of the distinction between morality and simple expediency. It is a part of the notion of Duty in every one of its forms, that a person may rightfully be compelled to fulfill it. Duty is a thing which may be *exacted* from a person, as one exacts a debt. Unless

we think that it might be exacted from him, we do not call it his duty. Reasons of prudence, or the interest of other people, may militate against actually exacting it; but the person himself, it is clearly understood, would not be entitled to complain. There are other things, on the contrary, which we wish that people should do, which we like or admire them for doing, perhaps dislike or despise them for not doing, but yet admit that they are not bound to do; it is not a case of moral obligation; we do not blame them, that is, we do not think that they are proper objects of punishment. How we come by these ideas of deserving and not deserving punishment will appear, perhaps, in the sequel; but I think there is no doubt that this distinction lies at the bottom of the notions of right and wrong; that we call any conduct wrong, or employ, instead, some other term of dislike or disparagement, according as we think the person ought, or ought not, to be punished for it; and we say that it would be right to do so and so, or merely that it would be desirable or laudable, according as we would wish to see the person whom it concerns, compelled, or only persuaded and exhorted, to act in that manner. (*UT* V, 14)

One point before we analyze this passage. Mill presents morality as the realm of right and wrong, duty and obligation. He thus ignores such things as supererogation, and his account is incomplete. But his point is to delimit the range of moral requirements, which is necessary if supererogation is ever to be accommodated. I shall ignore these further complications in (and possibly for) Mill's theory of morality.

As Mill suggests within this paragraph and makes clear within the next (*UT* V, 15), morality is a sector of expediency, as justice is a sector of morality. Mill says that we can negatively appraise conduct without regarding it in moral terms—without condemning it as *wrong*. An act may be inexpedient, undesirable, or regrettable, but it is not wrong unless sanctions are appropriate. Now, there must be some basis for appraising acts even when they are not be be counted as wrong, that is, within the part of expediency that falls outside morality. This is either (a) the principle of utility or (b) some other standard. There seems no reason to deny that utility would be used by Mill to judge the expediency of acts, or that the principle of utility is Mill's basic, most comprehensive standard for conduct; so (a) seems the more plausible interpretation by far. This indicates that Mill would wish to rank alternative acts according to their utilities (their instrumental value) but is not committed to calling an act wrong just because it fails to maximize utility. In order for an act to be wrong, Mill quite clearly says, sanctions must be fitting.

Thus, the very distinction between morality and expediency indicates that Mill is not an act-utilitarian. Note that, even if we chose (b) and imagined that the principle of utility governed only moral matters and not the whole of "expediency," we would still find that Mill is not an act-utilitarian. This is because of utilitarian constraints upon the use of sanctions, which I discuss below.

This allows us to see Mill as making much more moderate teleological assumptions than are usually attributed to him. On the act-utilitarian interpretation, Mill is committed to holding that one is always morally bound to produce as much happiness (or, abstractly, as much intrinsic value) as possible—the most extreme teleological position. On the reading of Mill that I am proposing here, he is committed only to ranking acts according to their utilities, and to preferring more beneficent to less beneficent acts. But that does *not* commit him to regarding a failure to maximize utility as morally wrong.

This way of reading Mill also sheds some light on his "proof" of the principle of utility, as least in clarifying his conception of the issue (see *UT* IV). Mill does not argue for a principle that speaks of right and wrong action. His principle concerns *ends*.[2] In a typical passage he says, "The utilitarian doctrine is that happiness is desirable, and the only thing desirable, as an end; all other things being only desirable as means to that end" (*UT* IV, 2). When he has completed the main part of his proof, he says, "If so, happiness is the sole end of human action, and the promotion of it the test by which to judge of all human conduct; from whence it necessarily follows that it must be the criterion of morality, since a part is included in the whole" (*UT* IV, 9). These accord with, and reinforce, my reading of chapter V. We can best respect Mill's words by allowing him, quite reasonably, to *value* acts by reference to ends without forcing him to say, implausibly, that acts *must* always produce as much value or happiness as possible, lest they be wrong. This is precisely what Mill seems to deny in paragraph 14 of chapter V.

The distinction drawn by Mill between morality and expediency is couched in terms that may seem further to support my case. For "expediency" might easily be taken in a utilitarian sense, as Mill sometimes suggests. This would accord with my view that the principle of utility is Mill's basic and most comprehensive principle of conduct, and thus

2. See also D. G. Brown, "What Is Mill's Principle of Utility?" *Canadian Journal of Philosophy* 3(1973): 1–12.

governs expediency as well as morality proper. I have not used this bit of evidence because I think Mill's argument is clearer and more interesting if we understand it differently.

I suggest that "expediency" is Mill's term for the evaluation of actions in general, neutrally described, that is, without assuming a principle of utility. The term would still come naturally to Mill, because of his teleological orientation. Mill assumes that conduct must be evaluated by reference to ends, and that utilitarianism is to be distinguished from other theories by its endorsement of a certain end—happiness. When Mill distinguishes between expediency and its proper part, morality, he is not invoking utilitarian values but rather seeking to sort out the relevant concepts. The distinction is drawn by referring to sanctions, which implies no commitment to utilitarianism.

There is a parallel between this passage and Mill's discussion of moral rights. Mill says, "When we call anything a person's right, we mean that he has a valid claim on society to protect him in the possession of it, either by force of law, or by that of education and opinion" (*UT* V, 24). This is neutral with respect to utilitarianism. In the remainder of the paragraph, Mill expands on his analysis. At the start of the next paragraph, he restates the point, in slightly different terms: "To have a right, then, is, I conceive, to have something which society ought to defend me in the possession of" (*UT* V, 25). This does not assume utilitarianism. His substantive commitment is clearly separated, and clearly presented, in the next sentence: "If the objector goes on to ask why it ought, I can give him no other reason than general utility" (*UT* IV, 25). Mill's utilitarianism provides the reasons to support such claims, not their analysis.

Mill's basic theory of morality and justice do not assume utilitarianism. That is why they are of potentially far-reaching significance. Mill does not offer us a form of utilitarianism that happens to acknowledge rights and obligations. Rather, he believes that moral judgments unavoidably concern such matters and thus that any theory ignoring rights and obligations is conceptually defective.

II. Morality and Coercive Sanctions

My reading can be reinforced and extended if we take account of the role played by sanctions in Mill's theory of morality. The wrongness of an act and the breach of a moral obligation imply something about "punishment," broadly speaking, which includes legal sanctions, social disapprobation, and guilt feelings. The wrongness of an act is not *conclusive* warrant for legal sanctions, but it does *imply* some warrant for some sort of sanction. Mill's formulations indicate that informal social sanctions may be justified when legal sanctions are out of place, and that guilt feelings are warranted even when public bad treatment is not.

If we try to combine this with the act-utilitarian reading of Mill we obtain the following view: the failure to do one's duty is wrong, and this implies that sanctions are prima facie justified. But our basic overriding moral duty says that we must always maximize utility. Therefore, the failure to maximize utility is a *sufficient* condition for a prima facie case for using sanctions.

It is implausible to suppose that Mill believed this. For it is a utilitarian platitude that sanctions involve disutility; even the "internal sanction" of conscience is assumed to be unpleasant. Sanctions therefore always require justification. But their justification is thoroughly contingent, for it is recognized that sanctions do not necessarily possess utility. Therefore, if Mill believes that an act's being wrong strictly *implies* even prima facie justification for some kind of sanction, then (assuming he accepts the observations just made) he cannot consistently believe that a sufficient condition of an act's being wrong is that it fails to maximize utility. A sympathetic reading of Mill would reject this notion. And so we have a second reason to reject the act-utilitarian interpretation.

This argument assumes that Mill's attitude towards punishment is strictly utilitarian. Now it would in any case be interesting to examine a utilitarian approach to morality along the lines suggested here by Mill. But we also have some independent evidence of Mill's approach to punishment. This topic was a focal point of Bentham's work, which Mill knew well. Mill appraised Bentham's theories on several occasions, but found no fault worth noting in Bentham's treatment of punishment, which was rigorously utilitarian. Instead, he wrote that this was one of Bentham's soundest doctrines, and that Bentham left the theory of punishment "nearly complete."[3]

3. John Stuart Mill, "Remarks on Bentham's Philosophy," in *Essays on Ethics, Religion, and Society,* ed. J. M. Robson (Toronto, University of Toronto Press, 1969), p. 11.

Mill says that punishment makes the difference between moral obligation and simple expediency. But "punishment" refers not just to legal sanctions. We have observed that Mill consistently implies, by his formulations, that even when legal sanctions cannot be justified, other sanctions may well be; if not informal social sanctions, then at least guilt feelings are fitting when someone does something that is truly wrong. Mill seems to be saying that wrong acts are those for which guilt feelings are appropriate. Punishment, in the usual, more narrow, sense, is not automatically warranted. When the stakes are high and additional grounds can accordingly be given, social measures may be justified, such as public condemnation and legal punishments. But these are added on, as the case demands. (See also *OL* V, 15.)

But how, exactly, do sanctions get incorporated into Mill's theory of morality? Here more elaborate reconstruction is necessary. Mill regularly associates "punishment" with such things as "compulsion" and "coercion," where it is clear that these notions concern threats applied *before* a wrong is done and not just physical restraint (see also *OL* I, 9–11). Mill seems to see punishments for particular wrongs, which occur *retro*spectively, and compulsion or coercion, operating *pro*spectively, as two sides of the same phenomenon. But the latter can be rational only if attached to clear guidelines laid down for future behavior.

This leads us to the Benthamic idea of *coercive rules* that require or forbid. There is ample evidence that Mill conceives of informal social rules (the elements of popular or conventional morality) along such lines (see *OL* I, 5–6, 9–11; IV, 3; V, 2, 15). And there seems no question that he conceives of legal rules in just this way; note Mill's comment that "the idea of penal sanction" is "the essence of law" (*OL* V, 14). Mill's references to sanctions suggest he is assuming they would be threatened by and applied under coercive rules.

In Bentham's view,[4] laws are meant primarily to regulate the behavior they require or forbid. In order to do so effectively, he thought, they must employ coercive sanctions. Informal social rules—the elements of popular or conventional morality—can also be conceived of as coercive commands and prohibitions. These are generally accepted standards for minimally acceptable behavior, whose existence is a matter of general knowledge before the acts they concern are contemplated or performed.

4. See David Lyons, *In the Interest of the Governed,* rev. ed. (Oxford: Clarendon, 1991), chaps. 6–7.

This means that they can function prospectively as "moral coercion" and that certain consequences of breaking them can be thought of on the model of particular punishments in law. The specific penalty most mentioned by Mill is verbal comdemnation in moral terms. It is important for him to emphasize this sort of sanction, because he wishes to distinguish moral condemnation from less emphatic disapproval, but he allows that informal social sanctions can take nonverbal forms (see *OL* IV, 5–6).

Internal sanctions are more difficult to construe upon this model. They are linked essentially not to social rules but rather to a person's own convictions. The latter cannot so naturally be thought of as coercive commands laid down to regulate behavior; having the requisite values seems rather to involve aversions to behaving in certain ways and the disposition to reproach oneself (as well as others, perhaps) for so behaving. But these differences can be exaggerated; significant traces of the legal model can be found here too. Such values can be conceived of as directives for conduct; the associated sanctions are undesirable consequences of noncompliance; it is psychologically possible to behave in certain ways to avoid a guilty conscience; the total mechanism is important in determining behavior; and the values can be affected in various ways, beginning with a child's moral education. Most important for our purposes, however, is this. Although personal values should not be confused with popular morality (since one can be a dissenter), there are close links between the two. Personal values are logically presupposed by—indeed they are constitutive of—popular morality. In a given group, most of the personal values of most people are likely to be shared. To some extent, therefore, both popular and internal sanctions can be thought of as attached to one single set of rules.

This may help to explain how Mill could talk of internal sanctions while employing a model based on coercive social rules. For there to *be* informal social rules, the corresponding values must be *internalized* widely within the group. Thus, the judgment that a certain set of informal rules would be justified implies approval of the same values being generally internalized.

This may also help to explain why Mill assumes that internal sanctions would justifiably operate though social sanctions may not always be warranted. Mill says that the wrongness of an act implies some warrant for punishment, though not conclusive justification for social sanctions. For when applied in particular cases these involve specific, controllable acts, whose justification does not follow from the justification for the existence of the general rule. To justify the rule is to justify the threat of punishment for certain acts, but this gives only a necessary and not a sufficient condition for the justified infliction of punishment in individual cases. The latter requires also that the rule be applied to the case in question, that guilt be determined, and (in the language of the law) that sentence be passed. This is a relatively formal process under the law, much less so within conventional morality; but corresponding stages can be distinguished in the latter realm as well. By contrast, the application of internal sanctions—guilt feelings for one's own acts—is more or less automatic (ignorance and self-deception aside). From the fact that an informal social rule exists, it *follows* that internal sanctions would generally be applied in the relevant cases. Any argument that justifies the existence of an informal social rule must be seen as an argument for the internal sanction to operate in the relevant cases.

These considerations suggest that Mill had the following view. To call an act wrong is to imply that guilt feelings, and perhaps other sanctions, would be warranted against it. But sanctions assume coercive rules. *To show an act wrong, therefore, is to show that a coercive rule against it would be justified.* The justification of a coercive social rule establishes a moral obligation, breach of which is wrong. Someone punished under such a rule ''would not be entitled to complain,'' since he would truly be punished for a wrong done (not for doing something that is merely unpopular or illegal). But social sanctions may not always justifiably be imposed in the form of punishment for a past offence, since there may be overriding grounds for refraining from that further act.

I have characterized Mill's theory so far in terms of justified coercive rules, without assuming that such rules could only be justified on utilitarian grounds. Bentham, of course, took a utilitarian approach to their justification, and I am suggesting that Mill did too; but that is irrelevant to the basic distinction between moral obligation and simple expediency. Mill could consistently acknowledge that someone who rejected utilitarianism could accept his theory of morality and apply it in the light of different substantive views about justification.

III. Morality and Utility

Let us now link this with Mill's utilitarianism. On Bentham's view, coercive sanctions have disutility, which includes the sanctions that are actually imposed as punishments for past offences, as well as the ''mischief'' that results from threatening such punishments. Any effective law involves unavoidable disutility, and stands in need of justification.[5]

To determine whether a possible law would be justified, or to appraise an actual law, one must weigh its costs against the benefits they purchase. A somewhat simplified cost-benefit accounting (which will serve our purposes adequately) works as follows. The benefits are extra utilities or prevented disutilities that result from the coercively induced redirection of conduct into paths that are collectively more useful than those that would otherwise be taken. The costs are those attaching, directly or indirectly, to the use of sanctions. A law is justified only when the benefits outweigh the costs.[6] Thus, the determination of a justified law depends not only on the utility of the behavior that is regulated but *also on the disutility of regulating it.*

A utilitarian would assimilate these conclusions as follows. From the fact that an act fails to maximize utility, or even causes positive, avoidable suffering, it does not follow that there ought to be a law against it. A utilitarian must have assurance that the benefits exceed the costs. Otherwise, he holds that there ought *not* to be a law.

Similar considerations apply to informal social rules, when they are conceived of as coercive commands and prohibitions. They may be justified, if their benefits exceed their costs. For such rules involve disutilities too. And thus it would be natural for Mill to hold that acts that fail to maximize utility are not necessarily wrong. For rules prohibiting them could not necessarily be justified.

We have seen why Mill might have thought that internal sanctions would operate in roughly a proper subset of cases in which informal social sanctions could be justified: the former operate more or less automatically, while the latter involve additional social conduct. Now, Mill also seems to assume that legal sanctions would be ''superadded'' to the others, applying in a proper subclass of the cases regulated by informal social sanctions. How can this be understood?

Mill might believe that legal sanctions are more difficult to justify than others, and so he might be taken as reasoning that legal intervention could be justified in a *smaller class* of cases; for the stakes would have to be higher, to outweigh the higher costs of legal sanctions. This is plausi-

---

5. Lyons, *In the Interest of the Governed,* chaps. 6–7.

6. That may do for the evaluation of rules in force but not for deciding between nonequivalent rules that pass the test. To the extent that such rules differ, one's moral obligations under Mill's theory would be problematic.

ble, but it does not follow that the acts that could justifiably be prohibited by legal rules are a proper *subclass* of the acts that could justifiably be prohibited by informal social rules (and thus generally by conscience). The former might overlap, without being entirely contained in, the latter.

And it is reasonable to suppose that the two classes of acts would only overlap. Many legal rules might well be justified on utilitarian grounds though it would not be useful to incorporate them into social or personal morality. Commercial and property law, for example, contain many technical rules that are of parochial interest and application. Laws that establish useful routines or guidelines for regular business practices would not usefully be internalized.

The interpretive difficulty here suggests another. On the sort of view that I have reconstructed so far, Mill may seem committed to the notion that any justifiable coercive rule, such as a justifiable legal rule, corresponds to a moral obligation. But this seems implausible. Laws that establish useful routines or guidelines for business practices, for example, do not give moral obligations.

These difficulties can be removed as follows. We began with the idea that wrong acts are those for which guilt feelings are appropriate, and added to it the further idea that wrong acts are those against which coercive rules could be justified. If we limit the latter by the former notion, we get the theory that right and wrong and moral obligation are linked essentially to guilt feelings. But these are appropriate only when corresponding informal social rules could be justified. Moral obligations are determined by such rules. The only *relevant* legal rules and sanctions are those within this sphere: legal sanctions may justifiably be added in some cases, when the stakes are high enough. Other justified legal rules are irrelevant for present purposes.

IV. Some Comments on Mill's Theory

A great deal of Mill's theory rests, of course, upon his ideas about the moral concepts. Mill's comments are rough and quick, in need of careful elaboration, which I have not attempted. It remains to be seen whether something like Mill's ideas could be sustained. I shall try here mainly to forestall some misunderstandings.

I have suggested that Mill embraced what might be called a "sanction'' theory of moral obligation, and this may seem objectionable. Bentham had a sanction theory, amounting to the claim that one is under an obligation whenever a coercive rule requires one to act in a certain manner. The rule need not be justified. This sort of theory—which is, understandably, found most frequently in writings concerned with the (somewhat technical) notion of ''legal obligation''—seems utterly implausible when extended or transferred to the ''moral'' sphere, where we consider, not the societal requirements laid down upon us, but what our obligations truly are, regardless of what society requires of us or believes. It seems clear that one can have an obligation (in the relevant ''moral'' sense) without there being any corresponding coercive social rule, and even clearer that coercive social rules do not all by themselves create ''moral'' obligations. Consequently, the sanction theory of obligation has a deservedly bad name.

But Mill departs from Bentham at this very point. He accepts Bentham's conception of social rules and Bentham's theory of their justification, but employs a different concept of obligation. My account attributes to Mill the idea that one has a moral obligation if a certain sort of rule *could be* justified. This neither implies nor presupposes that such a rule is actually in existence, that the obligation is in any way ''enforced,'' either by social sanctions or by anyone's conscience.

Mill's theory shares the spirit and intention of rule utilitarianism in its refusal to require that each act maximize utility. Although it is predicated on the end of happiness, it does not ''collapse'' into act-utilitarianism. This can be seen intuitively as follows. Act-utilitarianism allows free moral choice only when utility could be maximized in alternative ways. But Mill's theory would presumably allow more moral freedom, because it would be more useful to allow it than to eliminate it by means of coercive social rules. This is because such rules have costs, and under Mill's theory there are no moral obligations unless corresponding informal social rules could be justified on utilitarian grounds. In more circumstances than under act-utilitarianism, therefore, and not necessarily in the same circumstances, coercive social rules and thus Mill's obligations would only set moral limits to conduct, without telling one what to do.

The point might also be made like this. It has been argued that corresponding forms of act- and rule-utilitarian theories are extensionally equivalent.[7] But (assuming these claims are correct) the results can

7. Lyons, *Forms and Limits of Utilitarianism.*

easily be misconstrued. The extensional equivalence argument applies directly to theories that judge acts singly and as members of classes defined on utilitarian grounds, respectively. It can then be extended to cover a special category of ''primitive'' rule-utilitarian theories, the ''rules'' recognized by which are ghostlike directives having no necessary relations to real social phenomena. These ''rules'' are, in effect, derivative, second-order judgments about classes of acts, and can be as complex and subtle as utilitarian discrimination requires. Ordinary social rules are not like that, so rule-utilitarian theories that employ more realistic conceptions of social rules place limits, in effect, on their complexity. Or, like Mill's theory, they take into account not just the utility of the conduct to be regulated but also the utility of regulating it. Once *any* such limits are placed on the rules, relative to the rules employed by primitive rule-utilitarianism, the extensional equivalence argument no longer applies. Consequently, it does not apply to Mill's theory of obligation, which theoretically diverges from act-utilitarianism.

The problem I mainly wish to pursue now concerns the relation between Mill's theory of obligation and his commitment to utilitarianism. Clarity will best be served, I think, if I deal first with misplaced criticisms of Mill's position, turning later to the version that may cause Mill real trouble.

It may seem that Mill's theory of obligation is incompatible with his commitment to utilitarianism. For it might be thought that the latter would oblige Mill to permit direct appeal to the criterion of utility in each and every case, with the result that one's decision should always favor maximizing utility. Indeed, I have not said that Mill restricts direct appeal to the principle of utility; quite the contrary. But (it may be said) the upshot is that a utilitarian would either follow the principle and seek to maximize utility in each and every case, thus trivializing Mill's ''obligations,'' or else would find himself torn between the moral requirements of his basic utilitarian principle and the different directives of the relevant rules with their limited class of moral obligations.

This particular objection rests, however, on a mistake—the assumption that Mill's principle of utility itself lays down *moral* requirements. For only then would one suppose that a commitment to the principle involves a determination always to maximize utility. Such a conception of the principle is understandable today, when we are used to thinking of it in terms of right and wrong conduct. But, on my reconstruction, Mill's principle of utility says nothing about right or wrong. It speaks of ends, and is not seen by Mill as requiring that acts maximize utility. Mill's principle commits him to ranking acts on the basis of their instrumental value. This falls far short of a moral requirement that each of us always strive to maximize utility. That can be gotten from Mill's principle only by attributing to him the most extreme and implausible sort of teleological assumption, chaining moral requirements rigidly to instrumental value.

There seems nothing paradoxical here about Mill's theory. Its limited notion of moral obligation seems perfectly compatible with a broad, general preference for, or approval of, acts that maximize utility. Mill does not hold that maximizing utility is morally obligatory, that a failure so to act is wrong. That simply does not follow from his principle of utility. Nor would it be derivable as a specific obligation, since it would not be useful to impose that value (maximize utility) by means of coercive social rules. But one could still approve of and prefer such acts; similarly, one could regret that acts must sometimes be done—since morality requires them—which do not maximize utility, or even cause avoidable harm. It is, indeed, a common moral phenomenon to think some value must be sacrificed by conformity to moral requirements. The utilitarian can experience this, too; it is, in fact, familiar to one who realizes that the interests of individuals sometimes conflict, so that serving happiness generally may involve frustration or unhappines for some. In the present case, moreover, we should remember that the conflict is squarely between moral and nonmoral values (obligation and utility, respectively).

It may be useful to apply these observations to one sort of case that has widely been discussed—"freeloading." For present purposes, we can imagine the problem to arise as follows. Let us suppose that people are generally conforming to a justifiable social rule that corresponds, on Mill's theory, to a moral obligation. One has an opportunity to benefit by failing to conform, without detracting from the usefulness of others' conforming. Now, it could be argued that one would serve utility better by failing to conform, and infer from this that utilitarianism requires one to freeload. But Mill's theory does not have this sort of implication: such freeloading would simply be regarded as immoral. The utility of the freeloading act does *not* entitle one to infer that it ought to be done, that it would be wrong to abstain from freeloading. And the obligation says otherwise. The only *moral* judgment involved is given by the moral rule.

My discussion of this sort of case assumes that there are no conflicting moral obligations. Note that we cannot assume there must be one, for that would amount to the idea that Mill's theory implies an obligation to maximize utility. It does not strictly do so; and it is highly doubtful, as I have suggested, that such an obligation could be contingently derived from Mill's theory, since it would not be useful coercively to enforce such a value. More particularly, it is unlikely that there would be a moral obligation to serve *one's own* best interests. There would be no point in the corresponding coercive rule.

Of course, in slightly different cases, conformity to a justifiable rule would impose severe hardship on others or oneself. Mill is unclear how he would deal with such a case, though he gives some hints. He allows the possibility that obligations conflict, and he believes that moral obligations primarily prohibit various forms of harm to (as well as interference with) other persons (*UT* V, 33). Some such cases might therefore be construed on the model of conflicting obligations. But, in general, one would also expect Mill to recognize certain excusing conditions. He would not of course allow the mere endeavor to maximize utility as a general excuse; but he could acknowledge extreme cases of hardship imposed by obligations.

It should be noted that the principle of utility is sometimes used by Mill to determine whether acts are right or wrong. But the only cases that Mill clearly deals with in this way are those in which moral obligations conflict (see *UT* II, end). And, even then, he suggests that the principle would be used to rank the opposing obligations, not directly to determine the utility of the particular alternative actions (see *UT* V, 32–33). In such cases, apparently, our conception of the moral obligations would be refined (see *UT* V, 37).

Another sort of case that might cause difficulty arises when the relevant justifiable rules do *not* exist. According to my reconstruction, Mill holds the wrongness of an act to be a function of not only its own utility but also the utility of regulating it by means of generally internalized, shared social values. In this respect, Mill's theory contrasts sharply with some recent versions of rule-utilitarianism, which consider only the utility of acts to be required or prohibited and ignore the costs of such regulation. At the same time, Mill's view resembles many modern rule-utilitarian theories in that the relevant rules are (as it were) "ideal," not actual. Mill's theory refers to justifiable rules, but not just to rules that are actually accepted or "in force."[8]

If so, it might happen that, though general conformity to some informal social rule *would* be useful, the rule does not actually exist and so is not generally conformed to, and isolated acts of adherence to the corresponding obligation could amount to useless self-sacrifice. It could be argued that, while this may accord with Mill's theory of morality, it hardly seems faithful to the spirit of utilitarianism. Thus, it might be socially useful for people generally to resist an oppressive regime, but useless and exceedingly dangerous for individuals to do so in isolated cases. From a utilitarian point of view, useless self-sacrifice in the service of such "obligations" is irrational, since it can be seen to involve loss without any prospect of the gain that would be reaped from general conformity to such a role.

I am not sure that Mill seriously entertains the possibility of such cases in connection with his theory of obligation. This might be explained in two ways. First, he fails to work out the details of his theory to any great extent; I have gone far beyond the text in reconstructing it. Second, Mill often writes as if he assumed that our basic underlying values are essentially utilitarian—as if the development of civilization has involved increasingly useful shared social values. To the extent that this assumption is unwarranted, adherence to Mill's justifiable rules could waste one's commitment to the end of happiness.

But there is also some reason to suppose that the problem would be minimized, at least in Mill's view. He clearly believed that moral requirements would be maximally useful if they themselves were minimal. That seems a message of *On Liberty,* which urges the limitation of coercive social interference to the end of others' protection, and it seems compatible with the discussion in *Utilitarianism,* chapter V. Useful social rules would prohibit some forms of socially harmful behavior, but they would not go much further, save to require helping others individually and collectively in ways that are essential to the maintenance of a minimally decent social life.[9] And not all such rules would usefully be internalized. Thus, it is unlikely, on these assumptions, that any rules of

8. This is implicit in, e.g., Mill's discussion of moral rights (*UT* V, 6). It should also be emphasized that Mill writes mainly of obligations, not of rules; the latter have been incorporated into his theory chiefly by way of my reconstruction.

9 See essay 4.

moral obligation would require sacrifice of a purely speculative kind. Utility would sometimes approve such personal sacrifice, and would value those who are prepared to make it for the general happiness, but it would not require risky sacrifice as a general rule. It would be more useful to internalize values that would lead us to work more deliberately for the general welfare.

Unlike recent utilitarian theories, Mill's is not preoccupied with either acts or rules. Mill is committed fundamentally to the end of happiness, and thereby to *whatever* means best serve that end. All such means may properly be judged by reference to that end, without the appraisal of social rules being subordinated to judgments of particular acts (as it is under act-utilitarianism) or the converse (as under rule-utilitarianism).

It is perhaps worth emphasizing that, since things other than acts are possible means to the end of (say) happiness, practical decisions cannot even be analyzed adequately unless these are taken into account. Consider the individual case. Suppose a person wishes to serve his own best interests in the long run. He will find it best not to decide each case as it arises, but to lay down some guidelines for his own behavior. He may recognize some temptations to which he is susceptible, for example, and discipline himself to avoid them. He may want some hard and fast rules to follow, which he has sufficient reason to adopt without entertaining the possibility of ever reviewing them. In this way, he makes personal policies work as means toward the end of happiness.

Suppose, now, our prudent individual reckons soundly that his best interests in the long run will be served by working at some job or saving over a long period of time, with real sacrifice involved along the way. He may set himself specific tasks, but such a policy would still allow him to decide each time whether conditions warrant making an exception. He cannot predict beforehand what sort of special circumstances might arise, but rational plans would make allowance for such possibilities. At the same time, he must place *special weight* upon his secondary commitment, or else it will be emptied of significance. And, even though he might make exceptions to his policy to meet unexpected contingencies, his decisions to do so, as well as his more normal resolution to keep working hard or saving, make *essential* reference to his policy. It shapes his conduct over a period of time, it helps to determine which sort of behavior will be rational, and it even frames his questions when he must decide whether or not to change direction entirely. In these respects, the appraisal of his behavior as prudent or otherwise presupposes that such policies be taken into account. They are not eliminable. To look at his choices as if they concerned single acts undertaken separately would be a gross distortion of the relevant considerations.

A utilitarian like Mill should reason in a somewhat analogous manner. He is committed to the end of happiness, and to evaluating all other things that may serve as means to it accordingly. From this it does not follow that he requires each person always to maximize utility. What he wishes is for us to choose our means most wisely to serve the end of happiness.

An interesting example is given by Mill's theory of liberty. Mill believes that happiness will best be served in the long run if we restrict our deliberations concerning coercive social interference so that they are predicated solely upon the prevention of harm to people other than the agent whose freedom may be limited. Mill recognizes that this restriction does not follow from his general happiness principle, which could conceivably approve of, say, interference meant to benefit those whose freedom was to be limited. But he believes that we are bound to be misled by appearances, prejudices, or self-deception, and that the risks far outweigh the possible gains, so that we are better off restricting social intervention very severely. Thus, Mill lays down a principle that is supposed to hold without exception, even though it is supported only on contingent grounds by a more fundamental principle. In such cases, Mill believes, utility will best be served by following a secondary or subordinate principle rather than appealing directly to utility.

There is no paradox here, since in this case Mill is simply seeking the best means to the end of happiness. And it should be noted that such a principle cannot be construed as an act-utilitarian ''summary rule.'' It is not that we are most likely to do what we ought, in each particular case, if we follow such a rule generally, but rather that our *making it a matter of principle* to limit social interference in this way is an essential means to the end of happiness.

But this interpretation brings problems, too. As I am understanding Mill, he believes our moral concepts require us to judge conduct by reference to the utility of generally internalized, shared social values, whose costs are not ignored. At the same time, Mill's utilitarianism allows direct appraisal of particular acts. I have so far emphasized that these are logically compatible, because one sort of judgment is classified as ''moral'' while the other is not.

Even though these judgments may be logically compatible, one might still wonder whether Mill's commitment to happiness must be seen as taking precedence over his moral judgments. The latter lay down moral requirements that conflict in some cases with the end of maximizing utility. One might suppose that a commitment to morality is necessarily superior by virtue of the respective judgments, one of which involves an obligation, the other concerning only instrumental value. But, it may be asked, if happiness is really Mill's *ultimate* end, how better to express it but by refusing to subordinate it to *any* conflicting values?

It seems to me the solution to this problem is not obvious. Mill could modify his theory of morality, to ensure that it would never conflict with the maximization of utility, but this would fly in the face of his conceptual claims. Mill could adopt the recent fashion of characterizing whatever principles he is least willing to surrender as his ''morality,'' but his distinction between morality and simple expediency would seem to rule out such an evasion of the issue.

There are two reasons why I am uncertain which way Mill must go. I am uncertain whether his commitment to the end of happiness necessarily involves subordination of all other values. And I am unsure independently whether moral values must be supposed to take precedence over all others.

It may, perhaps, be a virtue of my reconstruction of Mill's theory of morality that it poses such a problem for Mill. One suspects that he never squarely faces such potential difficulties, but that he could be persuaded they are real and serious.

3

Mill's Theory of Justice

It is time we reconsidered the relations between justice and utilitarianism.[1] Thanks to a convergence of political and philosophical development, interest in political philosophy and the problem of justice is greater than it has been for many years. Significant contributions have recently been made to the field.[2] But our understanding of the political face of utilitarianism is, by contrast, rather crude. By reexamining Mill's theory, I shall try in this essay to help us gain a better grasp upon the utilitarian view of justice.

I

Mill begins chapter V of *Utilitarianism*, "On the Connection Between Justice and Utility," by acknowledging that "one of the strongest obsta-

This essay is a sequel to essay 2. An earlier version was presented at the University of Texas; I am grateful for the comments I received on that occasion. I would also like to thank Stephen Massey and Robert Summers for their comments and suggestions.

1. I explored somewhat similar problems from a different point of view in "Human Rights and the General Welfare," *Philosophy and Public Affairs* 6(1977): 113–29. For a different reading of Mill, see Jonathan Harrison, "The Expedient, the Right, and the Just in Mill's *Utilitarianism*," *Canadian Journal of Philosophy,* Suppl. 1, pt.1 (1974): 93–107.

2. See, e.g., Joel Feinberg, "Justice and Personal Desert," in *Justice: Nomos VI,* ed. C. J. Friedrich and J. W. Chapman (New York: Leiber–Atherton, 1974), pp. 69–97, and "Noncomparative Justice," *Philosophical Review* 83(1974): 297–338; John Rawls, *A Theory of Justice* (Cambridge, Mass.: Belknap, 1971); Robert Nozick, "Distributive Justice," *Philosophy and Public Affairs* 3(1973): 45–126.

cles to the reception of the doctrine that utility or happiness is the criterion of right and wrong has been drawn from the idea of justice" (1).[3] That obstacle remains: most critics of utilitarianism see justice as its Achilles' heel. Indeed, we tend to think of utilitarians as having no appreciable account of social justice, and thus as neglecting a most important aspect of morality. This is understandable. Mill aside, the classical utilitarians pay little attention to the concept and problems of justice—and what little they say often seems wrong. Bentham hardly mentions justice in his philosophical works (though he has much to say, of course, about the justification of punishment). Austin and Sidgwick appear to have an impoverished conception of justice as mere regularity or conformity to rule. Few recent writers have done much better on this score. More important, this general neglect of justice does not seem accidental. The principle of utility worries about such things as "plea-sure" and "pain," happiness and welfare; it says nothing about justice. It has been understood to require that one always "maximize utility," regarding any other way of acting as wrong, while ignoring what may be *due* a person and what one may have *a right* to or to do. Considerations of justice could not carry any independent weight in such a theory, so its neglect by utilitarian writers seems perfectly natural.

Critics of utilitarianism have not let the matter rest there. Social justice is understood by many to concern the "distribution" of benefits and burdens among persons, and critics have contended that utilitarianism suffers logical as well as moral flaws in this connection. A logical flaw is found in the utilitarian formula that requires us to serve "the greatest happiness of the greatest number." It is said that this directs us to pursue two distinct and incompatible ends. The "greatest happiness" criterion tells us to promote satisfactions and prevent frustrations to the maximum degree possible, without regard to how they are distributed among individuals, while the "greatest number" requirement says that we must spread benefits and burdens as uniformly as possible. But satisfying one criterion might conflict with satisfying the other. This shows (it may be said) that the formula is incoherent or, at best, that it has indeterminate implications.

It should be noted, however, that the "greatest happiness of the greatest number" formula is associated with utilitarianism chiefly

---

3. All references in the text of this essay are to paragraphs of *Utilitarianism*, chap. 5, unless otherwise noted.

through works published under Bentham's name (not all of which were actually written by Bentham). It is not used much, if at all, by Mill, and even in Bentham's system its status is questionable. Bentham's idea appears to be that, when we try to promote happiness, we are not always able to serve the best interests of all those who are affected by our actions. The most important conflict of interests, according to Bentham, is that between those in power and those who are ruled—the ordinary people, "the greatest number." Bentham believes that, as a matter of fact, happiness will best be served when we aim at serving the interests of the latter group, and so he came to use the derivative, nonbasic formula, "the greatest happiness of the greatest number." Of course, his factual beliefs may be mistaken. But that does not show that the basic utilitarian commitment to serving happiness is itself incoherent.

A critic may reply that this way of answering objections to the "greatest happiness of the greatest number" formula merely illustrates the utilitarian's neglect of "distribution." Faced with a choice between maximizing satisfactions and distributing them equitably, the utilitarian is theory-bound to choose the former. At best, he might strike a compromise with the idea of social equality by formulating his criterion in terms of maximizing the average per capita satisfaction level (rather than in terms of maximizing total satisfactions). But even this version of utilitarianism is thought vulnerable to objections. It is often claimed, for example, that utilitarianism is defective from a moral point of view because it condones unjust social arrangements. It is, after all, *logically possible* that enslaving some persons in some circumstances would serve the general welfare better than any of the available alternative arrangements. And, it is said, a principle with such implications must be rejected.

Utilitarians have not embraced such institutions. Some have referred to the phenomenon of diminishing marginal utility in arguing for social equality. And utilitarians have believed that happiness will best be served in free societies. But contentions of this sort are often dismissed out of hand—not because they rely on false factual claims, but rather because they turn on facts at all. This assumes, in effect, that facts are totally irrelevant to certain moral judgments. A utilitarian who tried to answer the objection by citing the actual disutility of slavery or of inequality would be accused of missing its essential point.

The objection has some interesting features. In the first place, it takes for granted that slavery could not possibly be justified, no matter what the alternatives might be. A normally sound judgment may here be overextended. If the judgment is derived from an assumed independent principle, then the question is simply begged against utilitarianism.

In the second place, it is difficult to see how facts can be excluded from the argument. If moral principles are not regarded as "self-evident," then they are subject to criticism and need to be defended in some manner. The only plausible arguments that I know of—such as Rawls's—make extensive use of facts about the human condition. And most general principles can be applied to the varied circumstances of human life only with the help of considerable information. Since facts are assumed relevant to the defense and application of nonutilitarian principles, they must also be entertained when we scrutinize utilitarianism. Until we have established some principles of justice on nonutilitarian grounds and shown that utilitarian arguments for them are ineffective, we must consider what utilitarians have to say about such matters.

In the third place, the objection assumes that the logical possibility that slavery will maximize utility shows that utilitarians regard slavery as morally permissible, at least in some circumstances. But, if Mill is a utilitarian, then this is mistaken. On Mill's view, I shall argue, nothing is shown to be right by showing that it maximizes utility; nothing is wrong simply because it fails to maximize utility. For Mill distinguishes between evaluations of expediency and moral judgments: the former concern utility, the latter obligation. To show that something is not morally wrong, we must show that it does not breach a moral obligation, and this is not a matter of maximizing utility. Mill also holds that justice is the most important segment of morality, involving the weightiest obligations, which correlate with personal rights. To show that something is not unjust, we must show that it does not violate rights. This too is not a matter of maximizing utility.

Mill's theories of justice and morality are found in, or can be reconstructed from, the last and longest chapter of *Utilitarianism,* which discusses justice. I shall explain those theories further by noting and interpreting the most relevant parts of Mill's discussion.

II

Mill begins his discussion of justice by observing that the feelings associated with justice are stronger than and different from those connected with mere expediency. This leads some writers invalidly to infer that considerations of justice are independent of utility. Mill proposes to dissect the sentiment of justice, these feelings, in order to undermine entirely this fallaciously developed theory (1–3). Mill accordingly embarks upon a study of the idea or concept, as opposed to the sentiment, of justice, in order to identify the beliefs that are fundamental to judgments about justice and the circumstances in which the feelings associated with justice arise. We are primarily concerned here with Mill's attempt to analyze the concept of justice.

Mill begins this attempt by surveying the central uses of the terms "just" and "unjust." His survey finds justice connected with rights, desert, voluntary undertakings, impartiality, and equality (4–10). But the survey yields no unifying hypothesis about the concept of justice. Mill turns to etymology for illumination. This leads him to discuss the idea of law and that of "punishment," which brings him back to the realm of moral notions (11–13). Mill then outlines a conception of morality in terms of obligations and of justice in terms of rights (14–15). After this, he is ready to return to the sentiment of justice (16–23). Following an important passage on the nature of rights (24–25), Mill thereafter concentrates on substantive standards of justice. He discusses some conflicting views about punishment, wages, and taxation (26–31) and then sketches very broadly the substantive principles of justice which, he claims, could be based upon considerations of utility (32–38).

Mill's discussion is complex, sometimes subtle, often confusing. His formulations are, characteristically, wavering and imprecise. But his analysis of justice, centered in paragraphs 14 and 15, is striking and suggestive. I proceed on the assumption that it is important to take Mill's official pronouncements seriously, and that it is more illuminating to see what sort of consistent utilitarian view might then be attributed to Mill, than to take the usual interpretations for granted and to decide that he is inconsistent or unreasonable.

Some general points emerge clearly from Mill's initial survey of "just" and "unjust" that should be noted at the outset. First, unlike many other writers in his tradition, from Hobbes to the present, Mill avoids embracing an impoverished conception of justice. He is, for example, no legalist: the "ultimate criterion of justice" must be independent of positive law (6). Nor does he confuse justice with mere regularity or conformity to rule.

Second, Mill recognizes rights that are independent of both positive law and merely conventional morality. These are rights that we may fail to respect and enforce, the ascriptions of which can be justified by appeal to valid general principles. These rights, which are referred to in his analysis of justice, he thus calls "moral rights." In recognizing them, Mill parts company with Bentham, whose abhorrence of political hyperbole provoked him to deny their possibility.

Third, Mill holds that the obligations of justice are (like other moral obligations) not "absolute" but can be overridden. The corresponding moral rights are accordingly not in principle inviolable. Now, few, if any, writers on the subject would basically disagree with Mill here, at least concerning the particular rights Mill identifies. But the point is important because it may seem to threaten the very idea of a utilitarian account of justice. For (it may be said) suppose Mill does talk about "moral rights" and "obligations of justice." Such talk is empty if his utilitarianism compels him to regard any right or obligation as overridden for the sake of a minimal increment in the general welfare level. This suspicion assumes that a utilitarian is morally committed to maximizing utility. I shall try to show that this is not a feature of Mill's utilitarianism. The principle of utility concerns values or ends. It is not, in Mill's view, a moral principle, for it does not directly concern moral rights or obligations. Moral principles are gotten by applying values within the constraints imposed by the moral concepts. Mill's views about the central moral concepts are thus crucial for his moral and political theory.

Mill leads us to his theory of justice in the following way. He speculates that the original idea of justice amounted to the idea of conformity to law. But as defects in laws were recognized, the concept evolved into the idea of what *ought* to be (rather than what *is*) law. This still does not express the concept of justice that we have today, for the standards of justice are understood to apply in other contexts, even when there ought not to be any legal intervention. "But even here," Mill says, "the idea of what ought to be law still lingers in a modified shape" (13). Mill holds that "the essence of law" is "the idea of penal sanction," so he links the idea of what *ought* to be law with *justified* punishment. As he makes clear, however, "punishment" is not limited to legal penalties; it covers the entire range of sanctions, external and internal, including public condemnation and the reproaches of one's own conscience. On this understanding, Mill observes that "punishment" for injustice is thought fitting, gives us pleasure, is what we like to see—in brief, is thought warranted (13). Now we have arrived, Mill thinks, at a distinctively *moral* notion. This is the idea of *conduct for which guilt feelings are warranted.* At first it looks as if Mill is going to say that this is the root idea of injustice. But he quickly observes that this expresses instead the more general idea of immorality, wrong action, the breach of moral obligation (14).

Mill has not yet differentiated injustice from immorality in general. An act can be wrong without being unjust, and we need another notion to account for that difference. So far as conduct is concerned, morality is for Mill the realm of right and wrong, which are functions of moral duty or obligation. But justice goes beyond these notions: ''Justice implies something which it is not only right to do, and wrong not to do, but which some individual can claim from us as his moral right'' (15). Some moral obligations correlate with moral rights, others do not:

> It seems to me that this feature in the case—a right in some person, correlative to the moral obligation—constitutes the specific difference between justice and generosity or beneficence. . . . No one has a moral right to our generosity or beneficence because we are not bound to practice those virtues toward any given individual. (15)

The obligations of justice are those that correlate with moral rights.

Some qualifications seem implicit in Mill's expressly stated views. Mill suggests, for example, that morally wrong action consists in the breach of a moral duty or obligation. But he also recognizes that obligations can conflict, that one can override another. He would presumably connect morally wrong action with the breach of a moral obligation somewhat as follows. Failure to meet a moral obligation is sometimes justified, that is, when the obligation is overridden by another. To act wrongly, then, is not simply to breach a moral obligation but to do so in the absence of an overriding obligation.

All of this applies to the obligations of justice, which correlate with moral rights. These obligations can be overridden, and the rights are not in principle inviolable. Mill would presumably qualify his analysis of injustice, which is given in terms of the violation of a moral right, somewhat as follows. The infringement of a right is sometimes justified, that is, when it is overridden by another right or even (Mill seems to envisage), in some special circumstances, by an obligation that does not correlate with rights. To act unjustly, then, is not simply to infringe a right but to do so in the absence of an overriding right or obligation.

So far, nothing has been said or implied about "maximizing utility." But Mill is usually taken to be an "act-utilitarian," who holds that any failure to promote happiness in the most productive and efficient manner possible is morally wrong. If that were Mill's view, it would deprive his talk of moral rights and obligations of any practical significance. They would provide no special considerations relevant to the morality of conduct. But that is not Mill's view, as can be seen from his distinction between morality and "expediency," which parallels his distinction between justice and morality (14–15).

As justice is a sector of morality, so morality is a sector of the more general realm of act appraisals that Mill places under the heading of "expediency." The distinctions are best made, as Mill suggests, by reference to negative judgments. An act can be wrong without being unjust; this is because injustice involves the violation of a right and not merely the breach of a moral obligation. Similarly, to call an act wrong is to imply that it is not merely inexpedient, but that it (unjustifiably) breaches a moral obligation. On Mill's view, this is to imply that "punishment" of the act (in the broad sense already noted) would be justified. Guilt feelings for it would be warranted; but guilt feelings are not necessarily warranted for other conduct that is negatively appraised.

Since, on Mill's view, moral right and wrong are a function of moral rights and obligations, we might say, alternatively, that they are governed by moral principles, principles of obligation (including principles of justice, which also confer rights). But what are we to say about expediency, or act appraisals in general? Mill presumably believes that they have some rational basis. Since they are the broadest class of act appraisals, the applicable standard should presumably be Mill's most comprehensive principle. That is the principle of utility. The principle of utility is thus not a moral principle; it does not itself determine which acts are right and which are wrong, which are just and which unjust. If it does so at all, it must do so indirectly.

How this might work is suggested by Mill's account of rights:

> When we call anything a person's right, we mean that he has a valid claim on society to protect him in the possession of it, either by the force of law or by that of education and opinion. If he has what we consider a sufficient claim, on whatever account, to have something guaranteed him by society, we say that he has a right to it. If we desire to prove that anything does not belong to him by right, we think this is done as soon as it is admitted that society ought not to take measures for securing it to him, but should leave him to chance or to his own exertions. (25)

To support the judgment that one has a right is to justify a claim about sanctions which do not merely secure a certain pattern of behavior (as in the case of obligations without rights) but which serve in particular to protect or defend the individual in a certain way. Mill goes on to say that he would argue for such claims by appealing to "general utility" (25). He thus sketches something like a "rule-utilitarian" account of moral rights.

Some passages in *Utilitarianism* do admittedly suggest a different moral theory. When Mill first expounds and defends utilitarianism against an array of objections and misunderstandings, he says that "actions are right in proportion as they tend to promote happiness; wrong as they tend to produce the reverse of happiness" (*UT* II, 2).[4] Even at the start of chapter V, which we have been examining, Mill refers to his "doctrine that utility or happiness is the criterion of right and wrong" (1). These passages suggest that the principle of utility directly determines the morality of actions. They are a bit vague on just how that would work, but they might be cited as support for the usual reading of Mill as an act-utilitarian.

If Mill were an act-utilitarian, his explicit, deliberate discussion of morality, in chapter V, would be, not just pointless, but positively misleading and inconsistent with that position. Mill's talk of rights and obligations would be empty, since ascriptions of them would have little or no significance for practice. We might of course be forced to this interpretation of Mill, but it is worthwhile seeing if he has something more interesting to tell us.

In Mill's most extensive discussion of the principle of utility itself, in chapter IV, he treats it as a principle concerning ends, not actions. In arguing for his principle, he is trying to prove that "happiness is the sole end of human action" (*UT* IV, 8). It may be said that this commits Mill to a certain manner of appraising actions—instrumentally, relative to the promotion of happiness. But the idea that happiness is the sole end of human action (or in more recent jargon, that it is the sole thing of intrinsic value) does not logically commit Mill to an act-utilitarian conception of morality. He may be committed to ranking acts relative to their promotion of happiness. But that does not commit him to regarding acts below the top levels in such rankings—acts that fail to maximize utility—as morally wrong.

---

4. Even here Mill distinguishes between the utilitarian theory of morality and "the theory of life on which this theory of morality is grounded." The theory of life is the principle of utility that Mill defends in 4; the theory of morality is the one under discussion, presented in chap. 5.

Mill might of course erroneously believe that his principle of utility logically commits him to act-utilitarianism, or he might have other reasons for embracing it. But does he embrace it? Chapter V answers this question by explicitly outlining a different conception: judgments of instrumental value correspond to judgments of expediency, not to moral act appraisals.

In chapter IV, Mill brings in the appraisal of conduct as follows:

> Happiness is the sole end of human action and the promotion of it the test by which to judge of all human conduct; from whence it necessarily follows that it must be the criterion of morality, *since a part is included in the whole*. (*UT* IV, 8, emphasis added)[5]

This is a puzzling formulation. It is clarified, however, by the account of morality that Mill gives in chapter V: *morality is a sector of expediency*. Considerations of expediency (instrumental value) govern morality— but not directly. That is because moral judgments, in Mill's view, concern the justification of sanctions. To judge an act wrong is to judge that sanctions against it would be warranted. In the case of social or external sanctions, this clearly involves conduct by people other than the agent whose conduct is being appraised. For social sanctions are imposed by others. Something of this sort applies to internal sanctions too, so far as their justification is an argument for internalizing values and thus for acts of moral education. And it is a utilitarian platitude (presumably accepted by Mill) that sanctions, or the acts providing or imposing them, have disutility, and thus require justification. As Mill also understands, from the fact that an act is inexpedient (does not maximize utility) it does not follow that those other acts (involving sanctions) would be justified; it therefore does not follow (on Mill's view) that an act that fails to maximize utility is wrong. Someone with Mill's idea that moral wrongness is essentially connected with warranted sanctions—especially someone who is also a utilitarian—would have clear reasons for distinguishing morality and expediency, or in other words for avoiding act-utilitarianism. As we have observed, Mill's view that happiness is the ultimate end does not logically commit him to an act-utilitarian conception of morality. The passages that I have cited are often taken as evidence that Mill identifies wrong action with the failure to maximize utility. But Mill does not say this, and his explicit account of morality conflicts with this interpretation. Consequently, it would seem worse

5. Mill's characterization of his ''doctrine'' at the start of chap. 5, just cited, comes soon after this longer statement. I suggest the former be read as short for the latter.

than uncharitable to saddle Mill with an act-utilitarian conception of morality.

Since Mill is no act-utilitarian, there are no apparent grounds for regarding his talk of moral obligations as devoid of practical significance. He would not require that an obligation be breached or be regarded as overridden merely in order to maximize utility. Given this, there is no reason to attribute to Mill the notion that an act is obligatory if and only if it would maximize utility. Mill holds that obligations can be overridden by other obligations, and we have no reason to understand this in act-utilitarian terms. Moral obligations are determined as well as overridden in Mill's system by some more complex utilitarian calculation.

Similar reasoning applies to moral rights. Mill maintains that moral rights correlate with a subclass of moral obligations, so he presumably holds that the conditions establishing and overriding rights are the same as for the corresponding obligations. Neither the claim that one has a right nor the claim that a right may justifiably be infringed can in Mill's view be established on act-utilitarian grounds. Mill's explicit account of rights appears to confirm this.

I have suggested that Mill has something like a rule-utilitarian account of moral rights, and that needs to be explained. Part of the explanation is, as we have seen, that Mill's moral theory involves the *indirect* application of the principle of utility to conduct; he is no act-utilitarian. Beyond this, rules enter into Mill's theory as follows. Rights and obligations are, for Mill, *general* considerations governing conduct. Since rights correspond to a subclass of obligations, it will suffice for now to concentrate on the latter. Mill's talk about sanctions indicates that he is thinking of them operating prospectively as well as retrospectively— they deter and dissuade as well as reprove and rebuke. They can so act only if they apply to classes or kinds of actions, not just to particular acts taken singly. As I have argued,[6] Mill appears to be working with a model based on ordinary social rules, except that the rules of obligation we are talking about here are "ideal" in the sense that they concern justified sanctions. Such a rule exists when the corresponding value is internalized widely. In that case, the people who have internalized the value will be affected by the promptings of conscience (the internal sanction) before and after the occasions they have for adhering to the value; they will also be disposed to exert pressure on others (the social

6. See essay 2, sec. II.

sanction) who deviate or threaten to deviate from the value. To justify the existence of such a rule is to justify the widespread internalization of the corresponding value. To argue for an obligation is to justify the establishment or maintenance of such an "ideal" rule.

The *analysis* of obligation that I am attributing to Mill makes no reference to utility. In this it resembles his explicit account of rights—both are neutral with respect to utilitarianism and alternative value systems. Mill claims, as we have seen, that valid ascriptions of rights are the conclusions of arguments of a certain type. These argue for sanctions that defend or protect the individual in a certain way. This analysis makes no reference to utility.

To use such analyses—to justify such a rule and thereby show that an obligation exists and, in a special class of cases, that a correlative right exists too—one must appeal to substantive values. Mill's utilitarianism becomes engaged here. For a utilitarian like Mill, to show that such a rule would be justified is to show that the various costs attached to moral education, guilt feelings, and social pressures are more than outweighed by the benefits to be obtained from the resulting effects on behavior. Such costs are not negligible, so an obligation is not proved merely by showing that a failure to perform as the rule would require amounts to a failure on the part of the agents to maximize utility in those cases. The stakes must be higher.

This division within Mill's theory between analysis and justification is important for a proper contrast between his view and ordinary rule-utilitarianism. The rule-utilitarian begins by formulating his basic principle as a moral principle, linking the moral appraisal of conduct indirectly to the promotion of happiness or welfare. A rule-utilitarian principle that might be confused with Mill's moral theory could be formulated as follows: an act is right if and only if it conforms to a set of social rules the widespread internalization of which would promote happiness.[7] That is not the way Mill's moral theory develops.

As his account of moral rights makes clear, Mill claims, in effect, that

7. A recent theory that somewhat resembles Mill's is in Richard B. Brandt, "Some Merits of One Form of Rule-Utilitarianism," *University of Colorado Studies Series in Philosophy* (1967): 39–65; see pp. 57–58 for a brief discussion of Mill. This paper is complemented by Brandt's "Utilitarian Theory of Excuses," *Philosophical Review* 68(1969): 337–61. Though I arrived at this essay's interpretation of Mill by considering Mill's remarks about sanctions and their relation to Bentham's theory of punishment, which Mill embraced, the development of my hypothesis has undoubtedly been stimulated by Brandt's significant work in this area.

the moral concepts provide schemas for evaluating conduct *from a moral point of view*. If one wishes to determine whether an act is just, one finds out whether it violates a right. To find this out, one asks whether that person should be defended or protected in a certain way, or whether something should be guaranteed to him. This is a question about a certain kind of ideal social rule. So far, nothing utilitarian has been said. In order to answer such questions, however, one must invoke substantive values, utilitarian or other.

On this view of the matter, evaluating conduct from a moral point of view *does not leave it optional* whether to take rights seriously. A utilitarian who failed to do so (an act-utilitarian, for example) would have a theory that clashed with the moral concepts. Such a theory would neglect rights, and this would neglect a certain class of obligations, and it is the breach of an obligation (in the absence of an overriding obligation) that makes an act morally wrong. To neglect rights and obligations as the act-utilitarian does is to confuse moral with instrumental value, immorality with inexpediency. Mill does not reach this conclusion by advancing a rule-utilitarian principle, however; he does so by considering the logic of the central moral concepts. His *basic* principle is thus a claim about ultimate ends or intrinsic value. To get to *moral* judgments, he must appeal to nonmoral values in the way mapped out by the analysis of rights and obligations.

Mill's moral theory is important, then, because it provides a significant theoretical alternative to *both* act- *and* rule-utilitarianism. The particular analyses of moral concepts that are suggested by Mill may be defective. Nevertheless, it may well be that correct analyses would have comparable implications, that is, would indicate how one can argue from nonmoral values to moral conclusions.

It is not obvious that this approach is sound. Many would undoubtedly reject it (especially those who maintain the utter independence of moral values). But it is not obviously unsound, either. It seems to me to warrant very serious consideration.

III

Mill sees justice as the realm of morality that concerns rights as well as obligations. So far I have mainly tried to show that this notion is not rendered vacuous by Mill's utilitarianism and that it is in fact based on Mill's ideas about the relevant moral concepts. Now I shall discuss some problems and other noteworthy features of Mill's theory.

Mill's Analysis of Rights

Mill claims that valid ascriptions of rights are the conclusions of arguments of a certain type:

> To have a right, then, is, I conceive, to have something that society ought to defend me in the possession of. If the objector goes on to ask why it ought, I can give him no other reason than general utility. (25)

The characterization of this sort of argument does not require commitment or even reference to utilitarianism. Of course, one cannot construct such an argument, cannot defend a moral right, without invoking substantive values. And Mill does not hesitate to say that he would ground such an argument upon utility. But the analysis itself does not identify or limit the values that might be used in arguing for such protections and thus, in Mill's view, for rights.

Some further brief comments are in order. First, since some of the things to which one may be said to have a right are things one may not actually possess, we should prefer, I think, one of Mill's various formulations to the others. It is not that one must have something (beside the right), possession of which is to be preserved, but rather that something (which one may not yet have) is to be "guaranteed" to one.

Second, Mill says this is or should be done by "society." As in his account of obligation, Mill does not restrict the guarantees to those of the law; we might rely on "education and opinion" without legal intervention. Given my interpretation of Mill's analysis of obligation, I suggest that "society" is involved in the sense that an argument for a right is an argument for the establishment and maintenance of a point of shared social morality. The internal sanction is still central, but the value is to be shared widely within the community.

Third, it would be difficult to give either Mill's analysis or his application of it an act-utilitarian interpretation. Rules play a decisive role in "protecting," "defending," and "guaranteeing" things. They are conceived of, in part, as regulating behavior in advance, not just as authorizing sanctions retrospectively. Such rules may be broken only for the sake of superior rights or obligations, never just to maximize utility.

Fourth, it seems reasonable to ask what differences Mill sees between the case of a moral right and that of a moral obligation without a correlative right. He seems to provide three different answers. When he first invokes the idea of a right, to explain the difference between justice and the rest of morality, Mill describes the differences (somewhat hesitantly, and rather crudely) from the standpoint of the person bound. He says that obligations with corresponding rights bind one, not merely to act in certain ways, as other obligations do, but to do so with respect to definite persons at prescribed times (15).

When Mill discusses the sentiment of justice, he refers to the hurt or harm that may be done to an individual (18–23). And this might be taken as implying that respect for a right always serves the interests of the right holder, at least in the sense that others refrain from hurting or harming him. But the evidence for this inference is equivocal, because Mill is trying to account for the sentiment of justice on the basis of antecedently existing desires to defend oneself and to retaliate. In that context, he would quite naturally emphasize hurt or harm. It would not follow that Mill thinks hurt or harm is always the result of the infringement of a right, or of an injustice. When he discusses the idea of a right and of justice (as opposed to the sentiment of justice), he prefers to speak of a "wrong" or "injury," which do not imply a hurt or harm.

Mill's explicit analysis of rights does emphasize the position of the right holder, without implying that he is merely an intended beneficiary. He is someone with "a valid claim on society" (24). This suggests that he is entitled to stand upon the right, to press it, to call for its observance by others, and so on.

Mill's analysis is vague, but it is not devoid of content. Of current views, it seems closest to the claim theory, which emphasizes the special position of the right holder. It is compatible with the narrower choice theory. And, as we have seen, Mill's discussion sometimes suggests a version of the interest or beneficiary theory.[8] It is not obvious that Mill is on the wrong track entirely. A fully adequate account of rights might well be used as Mill envisages—to determine the moral commitments of, say, a utilitarian.

8. For the claim, choice, and beneficiary theories, see, respectively, Joel Feinberg, *Social Philosophy* (Englewood Cliffs, N.J.: Prentice–Hall, 1973), pp. 64–67; H.L.A. Hart, "Bentham on Legal Rights," in *Oxford Essays in Jurisprudence: Second Series,* ed. A.W.B. Simpson, pp. 171–201 (Oxford: Clarendon, 1973); and essay 1.

The Superiority of Justice

Although the concept of a right may not make essential reference to an interest, it is not implausible to suppose that the rights we have involve interests. Mill indicates that the interests served by the principles of justice that could be defended on utilitarian grounds are by and large the most important:

> Justice is a name for certain classes of moral rules which concern the essentials of human well-being more nearly, and are therefore of more absolute obligation, than any other rules for the guidance of life. (32)

Foremost among these are the rules "which forbid mankind to hurt one another (in which we must never forget to include wrongful interference with each others' freedom)." For these are "more vital to human well-being than any maxims, however important, which only point out the best mode of managing some department of human affairs" (33). The primary obligations of justice correlate, then, with what we may call rights to security of person and to freedom of action.

Mill believes that these obligations generally take precedence over all others because they serve our most vital interests. But Mill's precise reasoning is unclear. Since he is not an act-utilitarian, we would not expect him to rank obligations case by case, considering the "expediency" of individual acts when obligations conflict; and there is no clear evidence that Mill would adjudicate conflicts in that way. It would seem to follow that he must rank rules on some more general utilitarian reckoning, along the lines of recent rule-utilitarian theories. But on this topic Mill himself is silent, and his thinking appears unsystematic.

The ranking that Mill perceives can to some degree be explained by differences between the two large classes of obligations. Obligations without corresponding rights can, he thinks, be met in various ways, in alternative situations. The obligation of charity, for example, is understood to require a general pattern of sharing, not specific transfers to determinate individuals. Such an obligation leaves more room for choice on the part of the person bound than does a debt, say, to a particular person. For that reason alone, it can more readily be overridden. For there will be other opportunities to do what it requires. By contrast, Mill says, the obligations of justice require us to act in determinate ways towards determinate persons at determinate times. That is an exaggeration, but the point would seem to have some validity.

At any rate, it seems reasonable for Mill to hold that the obligations of justice concern interests that are by and large the most important. As we have seen, the stakes must be higher than merely securing some marginal increment of utility if we are to justify an ordinary moral obligation on Mill's utilitarian reckoning. The risks and costs of sanctions must be outweighed by the benefits to be gotten from the rule. The stakes must be even higher to justify an obligation of justice, one that correlates with a moral right. For greater costs attach to these obligations than to those without corresponding rights. So they leave the person bound less room for choice, and they involve greater liability to both external and internal sanctions, as well as to demands by others on one's conduct. To justify a right is not simply to justify a requirement on others. It is to justify right holders to act in certain ways, to demand respect for their rights, to challenge those who threaten or infringe them, to be indignant and perhaps noisy and uncooperative when they are violated or threatened, and so on. Here, as before, considerations that have nothing especially to do with utilitarianism may be invoked to determine the utilitarian's moral commitments.

Fidelity and Justice

Mill begins his discussion of justice with a survey of central cases. These, we have noted, concern rights, desert, voluntary undertakings, impartiality, and equality. Later Mill maintains that the idea of a right is most central. He would therefore seem committed to recasting all of the initial examples in terms of rights and corresponding obligations. He does not do this explicitly. I will consider two of Mill's central cases here, beginning with voluntary undertakings:

> It is confessedly unjust to break faith with anyone: to violate an engagement, either express or implied, or disappoint expectations raised by our own conduct, at least if we have raised those expectations knowingly and voluntarily. (8)

There is a complication here that I wish to place on one side. It is doubtful that disappointed expectations can be assimilated to promises as Mill suggests. I may knowingly and voluntarily raise others' expectations about my future conduct without intending to commit myself to the relevant performances, without expecting others to rely upon me in that way. In such a case it is doubtful that my conduct constitutes any kind of undertaking. But I waive this point. Mill clearly means to limit such cases, and perhaps that can be done more effectively.

More to the point, it is doubtful whether all binding undertakings can be cast in terms of rights and obligations. There is, of course, a standard philosopher's way of doing this: if the undertaking is morally valid and binding, we say that the one who makes it is "under an obligation" that is "owed to" the other party, who acquires "a right" to the first party's performance. But it is unclear that every undertaking that has moral significance can be described in terms of rights.

Suppose I am invited to a large, informal social gathering. My presence is desired but will not be required. The host urges me to come. I say that I will, without meaning to mislead. At the last moment I decide to stay home—not because something morally more imperative has arisen, but simply because I believe I would not enjoy myself at such a party that evening. The original undertaking can be said to have some moral significance, because I said I would come. This is evidenced by the fact that I might later offer a simple, polite excuse for not coming after all. But it would be a strange obligation that could be overridden by my reason for staying home. Obligations aside, could it be said that the host *had a right* to my attendance? Did I violate or infringe a right by staying home? The host might be said to have a right to *expect* me at the party. But that is not a right to my attendance, nor is it the sort of right that I could be said to have violated or infringed by staying home.

Clearly, the terms we use to describe cases will depend upon the circumstances and the understanding of the parties about the stakes involved. As the stakes get higher and our image of the undertaking and its consequences becomes more solemn, it seems more fitting to ascribe a right to the host and an obligation to me. Let us change the example till we get a case in which the host might be said to have a right to my attendance. Let my presence be required. Once I give my word to come, the host acts in reliance on it. I cannot in good conscience deal with this undertaking as I dealt with the other. If I wish to stay at home, I should ask to be released from my commitment. If I fail to do that and fail to perform as promised, I am subject to some criticism. Perhaps it could be said that I would then have failed to meet my obligations; perhaps, too, it could be said that I have violated or infringed the host's right. But— and here is my main point—can we also say that I have done him *an injustice?* I find no plausibility at all in the suggestion. Fidelity and justice seem separate moral notions, the former not a special case of the latter.

This case is not peculiar. When we are not riding our favorite philosophical theories, we do not hesitate to speak of rights to life, to liberty, to security of person, and so on. Such rights can be violated or infringed—by killing, hindering and coercing, assaulting, stealing—but it does not seem to follow, nor does it seem to be true, that the victim is thereby done an injustice. He may be wronged, but not all wrongs against particular persons are injustices. Perhaps Mill is right in thinking that every unjust act is the violation of a right. It does not follow (nor does it seem to be true) that all violations of moral rights are injustices. If so, some principles that confer rights are not principles of justice.

This marks one respect in which Mill's analysis of morality seems too simple. But it does not necessarily represent a significant problem for his theory. If justice is simply a narrower category than rights, then if Mill can account for moral rights he would in the process account for justice. The rest would seem to be a matter of detail.

Desert and Rights

Many philosophers would seem to share Mill's notion that questions of rights are all questions of justice. On that view, fidelity might seem a facet of justice. By contrast, most philosophers would expect Mill to have trouble accounting for desert. Part of the reason, of course, is that principles of desert are often assumed to be independent of utility. But another part has to do with the scope of desert. As Mill understands, one can deserve either good or evil:

> Speaking in a general way, a person is understood to deserve good if he does right, evil if he does wrong; and in a more particular sense, to deserve good from those to whom he does or has done good, and evil from those to whom he does or has done evil. (7)

Mill later reiterates the point, in his discussion of equality:

> If it is a duty to do to each according to his deserts, returning good for good, as well as repressing evil by evil, it necessarily follows that we should treat all equally well (when no higher duty forbids) who have deserved equally well of *us,* and that society should treat all equally well who have deserved equally well of *it,* that is, who have deserved equally

well absolutely. This is the highest abstract standard of social and distributive justice, toward which all institutions and the efforts of all virtuous citizens should be made in the utmost possible degree to converge. (36)

There are two problems here. First, how can Mill recast this talk of desert in terms of rights? Second, how can Mill—as a utilitarian—endorse principles of desert? The two questions are connected. If he cannot construe questions of desert in terms of rights, then his theory fails or must substantially be revised. I shall concentrate on suggesting how Mill might recast claims about desert of the sort he endorses in terms of rights.

Mill endorses principles under which one can deserve bad treatment. These cannot be translated simply into principles about rights. For, whereas one can deserve either good or evil, the concept of a right seems more restrictive. It is paradoxical to suggest that someone has a right to bad treatment; and the apparent exceptions only reinforce the rule. Philosophers sometimes claim, for example, that people have ''a right to be punished.'' The idea seems paradoxical until it emerges that the right primarily concerns *eligibility for* punishment, not punishment itself. Being regarded as eligible for punishment is made to seem desirable, a good, relative to the alternative, which is being regarded as something less than a full person, something that cannot be held responsible for its behavior, something to be adjusted or manipulated.

If there is this difference between desert and rights, it follows that one who wishes to account for desert claims in terms of rights will have to deal with some desert claims indirectly. Where what is deserved is a good (e.g., good treatment by others), one can, perhaps, translate the claim directly into a right (a right to the good treatment). I see no insuperable obstacles here. But where what is deserved is an evil (e.g., bad treatment by others), the account must be more complex.

Consider, then, the possibility of understanding judgments about deserved bad treatment in terms of rights. When one acts badly, one may deserve bad treatment, or at least worse treatment than one would have deserved from those whom one has treated badly. The relevant moral relations might be characterized in terms of rights by utilizing the idea of *forfeiting* one's rights.

It might be held, for example, that one deserves special services or consideration from those one has aided in the past. Mill appears to endorse this and to regard it as equivalent to the claim that one has a *right* to such. Suppose, then, that I have aided you in the past but have since treated you badly. Before treating you badly, I might have deserved special consideration from you; after treating you badly, however, I no longer deserve that special consideration (or deserve it less, or deserve less of it). Mill might describe the situation by saying that, before I treated you badly, I had a right to special consideration from you; by treating you badly, by wronging you, I forfeited that right. The translation is not hopelessly implausible.

We can apply this sort of translation to the case of "punishment." We must begin with Mill's assumption that each person has a right to freedom of action and to security of person. Such rights correlate with obligations upon other people—not to interfere, generally, with one's activities, not to assault one, and so on. Unwarranted violations of such rights constitute what Mill calls "the most marked cases of injustice, . . . acts of wrongful aggression or wrongful exercise of power over someone" (33). I say "unwarranted" because no rights are regarded by Mill as "absolute"—not even these, which are supposed to rank highest in the scale of moral values.

Mill would seem to recognize at least three ways in which such rights are not "absolute," that is, in which hindering or hurting someone might be warranted. In the first place, such rights would initially be understood as *limited* in ways that are essential to their very existence. My right to act unimpeded by others, for example, would not cover acts of mine that are intended to impede others' freedom. (If I have the right to do that, it would be for other reasons.) In the second place, Mill allows the possibility that other rights and obligations take precedence in special circumstances. My right to act unimpeded could be *overridden* by, say, others' rights to protect themselves from my clearly dangerous behavior, however innocent my intentions. In the third place, I can *forfeit* such a right, at least to some degree, by my own bad conduct. My rights to act unimpeded and to security of person can be regarded as a right to generally good treatment by others—the kind of treatment that is required for a minimally agreeable sort of social existence. But this right can be forfeited by bad conduct on my part. If my conduct is sufficiently bad, then the stakes are high enough to justify external sanctions, including punishment. The use of such sanctions is, precisely, bad treatment of some people by others. But this bad treatment is nonstandard; it requires the special justification given by my bad conduct. In just such cases we may be willing to say, not only that I *deserve* such treatment because of my bad conduct, but also that I have *forfeited* part of my *right* to generally good treatment by others. These are the cases in which Mill would presumably say that one deserves bad treatment "from society."

Such an approach to at least a limited range of the principles of desert does not strike me as patently implausible or unpromising. Whether the argument can be substantiated in strictly utilitarian terms is a question I shall leave for another occasion.

4

Liberty and Harm to Others

The *principle of liberty* is not a simple corollary of utilitarianism. It is like a principle of utility in that it treats consequences for human welfare as justifying conduct. But it is narrower than a principle of utility, in at least two ways: it concerns harms to others, not welfare generally, and it concerns coercive intervention, not action generally.

Mill's principle of liberty is ambiguous in a significant respect, but Mill's applications of the principle help to clarify it. Critical commentary on Mill's theory of liberty has failed to note the relevant implications of Mill's examples; and as a consequence, much of that commentary presupposes a misinterpretation of Mill's doctrines. By reinterpreting Mill's principle, I hope to show that the principle is more acceptable than it might otherwise seem; but I do not pretend to offer an unqualified defense of it.

I. Mill's Principle

Mill's principle of liberty asserts

> that the sole end for which mankind are warranted, individually or collectively, in interfering with the liberty of action of any of their number is

Work on this essay was supported by a fellowship from the National Endowment for the Humanities, which I am happy to acknowledge. Earlier versions were read at the University of Calgary, Simon Fraser University, and the University of Washington, where I received many helpful comments. I am especially grateful to Jonathan Bennett, D. G. Brown, David Copp, Samuel Scheffler, and Barry Smith for criticisms.

self-protection. That the only purpose for which power can be rightfully exercised over any member of a civilized community, against his will, is to prevent harm to others. (I, 9)[1]

The prevention of harm to others is regarded by Mill as a good reason, and the only good reason, for "compulsion and control" of the individual, or, in other words, for the direction of behavior by threats, penalties, and force (I, 9).

In the course of his initial presentation of this principle, Mill offers some examples of interference it would allow. He begins with the obvious case: "If anyone does an act hurtful to others, there is a *prima facie* case for punishing him by law or, where legal penalties are not safely applicable, by general disapprobation" (I, 11). Not all such conduct should be prohibited, since there can be overriding reasons against doing so. Sometimes, for example, "the attempt to exercise control would produce other evils, greater than those which it would prevent" (I, 11). This suggests that coercive regulations are required by Mill not just to prevent harm, but to do so efficiently or economically. In any case, conduct that is harmful to others is clearly subject to control under Mill's principle. And one must suppose that the same is true of conduct that threatens to cause harm—reckless driving, say, as well as bodily assault.

But Mill does not stop there. The passage continues with other examples of justified "compulsion and control." Mill says:

> There are also many positive acts for the benefit of others which he may rightfully be compelled to perform, such as to give evidence in a court of justice, to bear his fair share in the common defense or in any other joint work necessary to the interest of the society of which he enjoys the protection, and to perform certain acts of individual beneficence, such as saving a fellow creature's life or interposing to protect the defenseless against ill-usage—things which whenever it is obviously a man's duty to do he may rightfully be made responsible to society for not doing. (I, 11)

I shall refer to these examples by saying that, in Mill's view, one may legitimately be required (at least in certain circumstances) to cooperate in joint undertakings and to act as a Good Samaritan.

These examples are presented by Mill as coercive requirements that

1. All references in the text of this essay are to chapters and paragraphs of *On Liberty*, unless otherwise noted.

would be permitted by his principle. D. G. Brown has argued, however, that they clash with it instead; and, partly for this reason, he has suggested that the principle of liberty is untenable.[2] Brown believes

> that we have duties to help other people which go beyond the avoidance of harming them; that the performance of such duties can legitimately be extracted from us, very commonly in our roles as citizens and taxpayers; and that such exactions are not permitted by Mill's main principle. (p. 158)[3]

Brown reasons in this way because he believes that Mill's principle of liberty does not allow interference unless the conduct that is interfered with can itself be considered harmful[4] to other persons. Such a principle would allow restrictions against bodily assault and reckless driving, for example, but it would not sanction either cooperation or Good Samaritan requirements.

Brown's interpretation of Mill is important because it forms part of a systematic study of Mill's doctrines, developed with reasonable charity. Brown furthermore avoids two errors that are commonly found in commentaries on Mill. He does not assume without question the textbook reading of Mill as an act-utilitarian, as one who holds that our sole or overriding moral obligation is to maximize utility. And he does not allow his interpretation of Mill's principle of liberty to get bogged down in discussions of Mill's distinction between ''self-regarding'' conduct (a term used by Mill) and ''other-regarding'' conduct (a term not used by Mill). Brown considers Mill's actual statement of the principle as well as his substantive applications of it. I believe, however, that Brown is mistaken about Mill's views on several important points, and I shall here defend a different reading of the principle of liberty.

On the reading I propose, freedom may be limited only for the purpose of preventing harm to other persons, but the conduct that is interfered with need not itself be considered harmful or dangerous to others. Such a principle both conforms to Mill's definitive statement and accommodates his examples. The cooperation and Good Samaritan re-

2. D. G. Brown, ''Mill on Liberty and Morality,'' *Philosophical Review* 81(1972): 133–58.

3. All simple page references within parentheses are to Brown, ''Mill on Liberty and Morality.''

4. Or at least he believes it does not allow interference unless the conduct is *dangerous;* see Brown, ''Mill on Liberty and Morality,'' p. 135, n. 2.

quirements that Mill refers to could not be justified on the ground that they prevent conduct that causes harm to others; but it can be argued that such regulations nevertheless work in other ways to prevent harm to others. This version of Mill's principle is one that he could readily endorse. It does justice to his own intentions and stays within the limits of his general position on morality and politics. Most importantly, it seems a more plausible principle than the one that Brown attributes to Mill, and one to be preferred by someone who accepts the idea that harm prevention justifies ''compulsion and control.'' But I shall stop short of claiming unequivocally that this principle is what Mill must have had in mind. The test suggests that Mill is, in fact, confused about some of the relevant differences between these versions of his principle of liberty and fails to face these issues squarely.

My argument proceeds as follows. In section II I discuss the differences between Brown's version of the principle and mine and show how Mill's examples can be accommodated. In section III I consider the problem of deciding which version best fits Mill's text. In section IV I go beyond Brown's argument and deal with other difficulties for the reading I propose, including other reasons for thinking that Mill's own examples cannot be accommodated.

II. Harm Prevention

Mill's principle, we have seen, allows interference with conduct that is itself harmful or dangerous to others, such as bodily assault and reckless driving. So much is certain. But harm to others is not preventable only by interfering with acts that can be said to cause, or that threaten to cause, harm to other persons, and the other possibilities are extremely important.

Consider Good Samaritan requirements. When someone has been injured or is in danger, harm (or further harm) to him might be averted if another person comes to his aid. It makes no difference here what, if anything, can be said to cause the harm or danger. If the principle of liberty says flatly (as on my reading it does) that the prevention of harm to others justifies interfering with my liberty, then it might justify interfering with my liberty in this sort of case. I might be required to come to another's aid, in order to prevent harm to him, even if I may not be said to have caused the harm that he will suffer if I should fail to help him when I can. In such cases, it cannot be assumed that someone who fails to help prevent harm can be said to cause the harm. Suppose, for example, that I am in a position to save a drowning man. If I fail to do so, I will have failed to prevent harm to him. But it does not follow that my failure can be said to cause the harm. For, as Brown observes, the drowning man may have tried to take his own life or may have been pushed by a third party (p. 145), in which cases the harm done would not be attributable to me, even though I failed to intervene. In sum, lives can be saved and injuries minimized—harm to others can be prevented—not only by interfering with, preventing, or otherwise suppressing harmful and dangerous conduct but also by requiring or otherwise eliciting helpful, harm-preventing conduct. This would seem to be the very point of one class of Mill's examples, in which we would be required "to perform certain acts of individual beneficence, such as saving a fellow creature's life or interposing to protect the defenseless against ill-usage."

Brown formulates Mill's principle of liberty as follows:

(L) The liberty of action of the individual ought *prima facie* to be interfered with if and only if his conduct is harmful to others. (p. 135)

In other words, there is only one good reason for interfering with a person's conduct, namely, that the conduct is harmful (or dangerous) to others. This may be called a *harmful conduct prevention principle*. It does not allow interference except with conduct that causes (or at least threatens) harm to others. It would not sanction Good Samaritan requirements.

Mill's definitive statement of his principle is not so restricted. It can be understood to say,

(L*) The prevention of harm to other persons is a good reason, and the only good reason, for restricting behavior.

This may be called a *general harm prevention principle*. It would not exclude Good Samaritan requirements. Someone who believes that there may be circumstances in which one may justifiably be required to come to others' aid, even though one is not responsible for their difficulties, should prefer a general harm prevention principle, like (L*), to a narrower harmful conduct prevention principle, like (L).

Another important class of cases is represented by cooperation requirements. Like Good Samaritan requirements, these would not normally be thought of as interfering with conduct that causes harm to others. But these are unlike Good Samaritan requirements, and thus warrant separate treatment, because they typically require acts that would not normally be credited, at least in the same direct way, with preventing harm. The prevention of harm to others here is more a function of the requirements themselves or of the patterns of behavior they create. Furthermore, in many such cases, each member of the community stands to benefit from the regulations—oneself as well as others, though only the benefits to others are relevant in justifying restrictions on one's conduct under the principle of liberty.[5]

Consider Mill's example of being required to give testimony in court. How is harm prevented here? It is true that giving testimony in compliance with a subpoena can sometimes be credited with preventing harm to others, as when it secures for someone an acquittal against a criminal charge or a successful defense against a damage claim. But it is unlikely that Mill meant or we would want to limit a subpoena rule to just such cases. One would presumably wish it to apply (as it does now), for example, to prosecution witnesses in a criminal proceeding. Compliance with a general subpoena rule can just as readily have the opposite effect upon the individuals who are most directly involved—by securing a conviction, say, or ensuring a successful damage claim. The harm prevention grounds for such a rule would not be like the case for Good Samaritan requirements.

If the requirement that one give testimony in court can be justified in harm prevention terms, it is likely to be by reasoning of the following sort. Courts, though costly and burdensome, are needed to settle and prevent disputes and for an effective system of social regulations. Courts are needed to prevent evils that are worse than the evils they entail. (For simplicity, we should assume that the substantive rules to be enforced can themselves be justified in harm prevention terms. Otherwise, a harm prevention defense of court rules and operations would have to be qualified severely.) Various rules are required if courts are to operate effectively. One of these requires persons under certain circumstances to give testimony. It is needed as part of an institution that helps to prevent

5. The relevant benefits are, of course, "negative," the prevention of danger or harm. For present purposes I assume, along with Mill, a distinction between the mere failure to secure some "positive" benefit and harm; but I shall return to this point.

harm. It might thus be justified on the basis of harm prevention, even though it cannot plausibly be treated as the prohibition of harmful or dangerous conduct. For the point of such a rule is not to interfere with conduct that would independently be characterized as harmful or dangerous to others, but is rather to channel behavior so as to help create or maintain a social practice that will help prevent harm.

In this sort of case, the harm to be prevented may well be "public," that is, presumably affecting all the members of a community, neighborhood, or class, at least in the form of danger or insecurity. This means that one may very well stand to benefit from the regulation of one's own behavior. Benefits to oneself (even "negative" benefits) are, of course, irrelevant to the justification of a rule under the principle of liberty. But, from the fact that the harm is public it follows not only that one stands to benefit but also that others benefit too, and this fact makes it possible to justify such regulations under that principle.

I do not wish to place great emphasis on the distinction between cooperation and Good Samaritan requirements. In the latter case, it is natural to think of one person's directly helping another by, say, removing him from danger or administering first aid, while in the former case one thinks of behavior within complex institutional settings or of coordination among a number of individuals, where one person's efforts could not possibly prevent the harm in question. But intermediate or mixed cases are clearly possible. For example, the coordinated efforts of a number of persons, perhaps within an institutional setting, may be needed to help a drowning, trapped, injured, or ill person. The contrast between cooperation and Good Samaritan requirements is useful here chiefly to suggest a variety of ways in which conduct may be regulated to prevent harm to other persons. It is not meant to suggest a sharp dichotomy or an exhaustive catalogue of cases.

It should also be emphasized that we are speaking here only of preventing harm and not of using coercion to promote benefits in general. One might object to the latter while accepting the former. Now, if one is concerned with preventing harm and believes that harm prevention may justify interference with an individual's freedom of action, then one should regard cooperation requirements as important cases. For they may well provide the *only* means of preventing or eliminating some significant harms, such as malnutrition and starvation, emotional disturbances, illness and disease, vulnerability to attack, homelessness, and so on. In fact, it is difficult to think of major social problems that might be dealt with just by limiting conduct that causes or threatens to cause harm to others. A principle that excluded other ways of preventing or eliminating harm would restrict such efforts very seriously.

Before concluding this part of the discussion, we might consider some examples that Brown himself proposes. He says:

> There can be no guarantee that joint works necessary to the interest of society will not include institutional care for the mentally defective, urban redevelopment, or foreign aid to countries whose economic conditions might otherwise lead to war. I cannot see how refusal to co-operate in such efforts toward alleviation of existing problems could be shown to constitute causing harm to others. (p. 146)

The last remark makes clear the context of these examples: Brown is claiming that what I am calling cooperation requirements cannot be reconciled to a harmful conduct prevention principle, that is, to Mill's principle of liberty on Brown's reading of it. I grant that point. But now the question arises whether they can be reconciled to a broader harm prevention principle. The short answer to this question is, it all depends. It is plausible to suppose that foreign aid for the purpose of preventing war could be justified on grounds of harm prevention; but other examples will depend more clearly on circumstances that are variable. To take one example: urban redevelopment, as I have seen it in New York City and Boston, could not always be so justified, since it is often used not to prevent or eliminate harms to others but to provide greater comforts and conveniences for relatively comfortable members of society while it actually undermines the conditions of those who are displaced and ignores their unmet basic needs.

I suggest, therefore, that the general harm prevention version of the principle of liberty is more plausible than the narrower harmful conduct prevention version. Furthermore, it appears that the former can, while the latter cannot, account for Mill's own examples.

III. Problems of Interpretation

Mill's definitive statement of his principle of liberty supports the general harm prevention reading, since it predicates interference on the prevention of harm to others and does not require that it be limited to the prevention of conduct that causes harm. Mill's own examples seem to accord with a general harm prevention principle, though they clash with the narrower harmful conduct prevention principle attributed to Mill. Can we then conclude that (L*) is closer than (L) to Mill's evident intentions? Mill does not permit us this luxury.

Brown thinks it clear that Mill means (L) and not (L*). He says, "Mill consistently writes and argues as if he had specified, not that interference with the conduct should prevent harm to others, but rather that the conduct itself should be harmful to others" (p. 135). One cannot deny that Mill's words sometimes imply this and thus support Brown's reading. My purpose in this section is to emphasize that the evidence is equivocal.

I have already offered reasons for the general harm prevention reading of Mill's principle. Evidence on the other side includes a number of passages which suggest the narrower harmful conduct prevention principle. For example, in the very paragraph in which Mill gives his definitive statement, he says that, to justify threats or penalties against a person, "the conduct from which it is desired to deter him must be calculated to produce evil to someone else" (I, 9). Indeed, his use of the term "self-protection" in the general statement of the principle might be taken as suggesting the narrower reading.

But Brown's reasons for ascribing (L) rather than (L*) to Mill do not end with such evidence. They also turn upon the following line of argument. Immediately after Mill offers his cooperation and Good Samaritan examples, he says, "A person may cause evil to others not only by his actions but by his inaction, and in either case he is justly accountable to them for the injury" (I, 11). This suggests that Mill mistakenly regards those requirements as equivalent to prohibitions against conduct that causes harm to others: if one fails to comply with them, one causes harm, not by one's act, but by one's omission, or "inaction." Brown argues that Mill would have no reason to suggest such a thing—to conflate failing to prevent harm with causing harm (by inaction)—unless he wished to assure his readers that the examples do not clash with his principle, which then must be understood to allow interference only with conduct that causes harm to others.

Brown then suggests that Mill is obliged to do this because of his other doctrinal commitments. The one emphasized by Brown is Mill's endorsement of a *principle of enforcing morality,* which can be understood as follows:

(M) The liberty of action of the individual ought *prima facie* to be interfered with if and only if his conduct is *prima facie* morally wrong. (p. 148)

Thus, when Mill accepts a specific duty, he is committed to its enforcement. But Mill's examples represent his acceptance of "duties to help people which go beyond the avoidance of harming them" (p. 158). The result is an uncomfortable predicament for Mill, which he resolves by misdescribing his examples, imagining that they fall within the limits of his principle of liberty. Brown concludes that "Mill has achieved consistency at the cost of truth" (p. 133).

The attribution of (L) to Mill thus forms part of a significant systematic interpretation of Mill's doctrines, a scholarly effort to which I cannot do justice here. I must confess I have strong reservations about Brown's claim that "Mill believes in the enforcement of morality," at least as a characterization of Mill's position in *Utilitarianism*, on which Brown relies.[6] But, in any case, Brown cannot defend his reading of Mill's principle by claiming that the principle of enforcing morality accounts for either Mill's examples or the predicament in which, on Brown's interpretation, Mill finds himself; nor can he claim that "Mill has achieved consistency at the cost of truth." The principle of enforcing morality does not tell us what our duties are; it simply commits one who holds it to the enforcement of whatever duties we happen to have. It is therefore incapable of explaining why Mill believes that we have duties to cooperate in joint undertakings and to act as good Samaritans. This is especially embarrassing for Brown's consistency claim. For, on Brown's reading, Mill is committed not just to (L) and (M), which can be understood as compatible,[7] but also to those troublesome examples. Mill's acceptance of the duties to cooperate and to be a Good Samaritan can be explained in either of two ways. It might rest on some further doctrine (beyond (L) and (M)) or else it might represent Mill's independent moral judgment, in which case it can be thought of as a doctrine in

6. The relevant passage is *Utilitarianism*, ch. V, par. 14. For my interpretation, see essay 2.

7. Since the principle of liberty purports to tell us the sole valid ground for coercive intervention, the principle of enforcing morality must be understood to say not that immorality is itself a justification for interference but rather that there is some such justification whenever conduct is wrong. It is therefore somewhat misleading for Brown to say that "Mill believes in the enforcement of morality" p. 146.

itself. Either way, it clashes, on Brown's account, with (L) and (M). For Mill is seen by Brown as committed (a) to certain "duties to help other people which go beyond the avoidance of harming them" and (b), by virtue of the principle of enforcing morality, to their enforcement, while (c) their enforcement is incompatible with his principle of liberty. On this reconstruction, Mill's position is untenable, and he cannot achieve consistency without a change of doctrine. He does not achieve consistency but merely papers over his embarrassment by misconstruing his own examples, thus sacrificing truth along with consistency. Furthermore, Brown's straightforward exposure of Mill's misdescriptions suggests that Mill exercises a considerable capacity for self-deception. These results are less generous to Mill than Brown may well intend. In any case, they should lead us to investigate alternative interpretations of Mill's doctrines.

On my account, no special explanation is required for Mill's cooperation and Good Samaritan examples, since they are accommodated by his principle of liberty. Mill faces no inconsistencies. And he endorses the most plausible principle of the type he is evidently defending.

So much for the larger questions raised by Brown's systematic reading. Let us return, now, to the most directly relevant text, Mill's own commentary on his examples. As we have seen, just after Mill presents his troublesome illustrations, he observes, "A person may cause evil to others not only by his actions but also by his inaction, and in either case he is justly accountable to them for the injury" (I, 11). But this is not the end of his commentary. Brown quotes the rest, but sees no further point in it. Here is how it continues:

> The latter case, it is true, requires a much more cautious exercise of compulsion than the former. To make anyone answerable for *doing evil* to others is the rule; to make him answerable for *not preventing evil* is, comparatively speaking, the exception. Yet there are cases clear enough and grave enough to justify that exception. (I, 11; emphasis added)

This passage shows that Mill acknowledges the very distinction that, on Brown's reading, he is supposed to neglect—between conduct that causes harm and conduct that fails to prevent harm to others. Furthermore, in employing the distinction as he does, Mill seems to be saying that he would allow interference not just to inhibit harmful conduct but also to elicit acts that prevent harm to others.

In other words, the evidence offered by this passage is equivocal.

Mill's initial comment on causing evil by inaction suggests some confusion about the character of his own examples, as if he wishes to limit interference to conduct that causes harm to others. In the continuation of the passage, however, he implies that interference to conduct that does not cause harm, but that fails to prevent harm, can be permitted by his principle, as his Good Samaritan examples require.

It should be observed that Mill's comments make no special allowance for cooperation requirements. From his silence on the matter, one might infer that Mill regards them as equivalent to Good Samaritan requirements—as if answering a subpoena were like saving a drowning person's life. That seems untenable. The failure to comply with cooperation requirements does not amount to such a simple failure to prevent harm to others. Indeed, it may have no effect at all upon harm prevention.

Suppose that cooperation requirements are justified because they are instrumental in preventing public harms, such as social insecurity and polluted air. We can then assume that each person in the community has a stake in the effective operation of the rules and therefore in compliance that is sufficiently widespread to make the joint undertaking effective. But we cannot infer from this that any single act of noncompliance places some relevant interest of some other individual at risk; a single act of noncompliance cannot be assumed to undermine harm prevention efforts.[8] It might, but then again it might not; and it is at least conceivable that one should know when a single isolated act of noncompliance will have no such consequences. Suppose, for example, that certain substances are dangerous only when they reach a critical concentration in the atmosphere. A pollution control rule might prohibit any release of such substances into the atmosphere, or it might try to reduce the frequency of such acts or the amounts of chemicals released, on the understanding that concentrations of that substance in the atmosphere below the critical level are entirely innocuous. Suppose, however, that an efficiently economical pollution control rule prohibits any release of the substance into the atmosphere, simply because it would in fact be practically impossible to administer any less rigorous rule. It might then be the case that some particular person on at least one occasion could know that his release of a small quantity of the chemical into the atmosphere will be an ·isolated act of noncompliance with the rule and that the

8. I discuss this aspect of thresholds in *Forms and Limits of Utilitarianism,* chap. 3.

harmful concentration will never be reached. His act of noncompliance might have no effect on harm prevention efforts and thus could not be assimilated to the failure to save a drowning man.

It must be admitted, however, that such cases may in fact be rare or even nonexistent. And, when one is reasoning about such matters probabilistically, with an eye on large-scale social engineering, there is a natural temptation to assume that we are never in a position absolutely to rule out such effects of noncompliant acts. One might then conclude that the relevant interests of each member of the community are put to risk by any violation of the rules. If there is an error here, it should not be exaggerated. One who reasons in this way need not suppose that a single act of noncompliance causes harm to others, or even that it straightforwardly fails to prevent harm in the way that failing to save a drowning man fails to prevent harm. He need only suppose that there is always, in such a case, some risk that harm prevention efforts will be adversely affected. One who reasons in this way might tend to assimilate cooperation requirements to Good Samaritan requirements. This might help to explain why Mill fails to give separate treatment to cooperation examples.

But all of this is highly speculative and we are left, in any case, with the impression that Mill fails to appreciate the complexity of his own commitments. There is clear evidence that he wishes to allow interference not only to inhibit conduct that causes harm to others but also to elicit harm-preventing conduct, broadly construed. At the same time, there is evidence that Mill tends to back off from this commitment or else does not fully recognize the theoretical decision that he faces.

IV. Benefits and Fairness

I have accepted Brown's claim that a harmful conduct prevention principle cannot accommodate cooperation or Good Samaritan requirements. Brown would, I think agree in turn with one of my claims, namely, that Good Samaritan requirements can plausibly be reconciled with a general harm prevention principle. But he appears to reject the idea that such a principle could also accommodate cooperation requirements. He says that "the general prevention of harm would not stretch to cover a fair share of every joint work necessary to the interest of society" (p. 146). He gives no defense or explanation for this assertion. One can imagine, however, why cooperation requirements might be thought incompatible with a harm prevention principle. One reason might be the notion that such requirements are in fact predicated on promoting benefits beyond mere harm prevention. Another concerns Mill's references to "fair shares." I will deal with these in turn.

The distinction between increasing benefits generally and merely preventing or eliminating harms is taken for granted by Mill. He assumes that some benefits would go beyond harm prevention and thus that their promotion could not serve in the justification of enforced requirements. This point requires some further explanation.

It might be assumed that Mill, as a utilitarian, should be understood in effect as following today's fashion in such matters and count the satisfaction of an existing preference as a benefit and its frustration as a harm. Mill's talk of "pleasures" and "pains" might easily suggest this. But important features of his moral and political doctrines, especially those concerning justice and liberty, seem to imply the following sort of view. While it is easy to be mistaken about what constitutes a positive benefit to another person, harms are unproblematic. Harms thus concern interests that are readily appreciated; most if not all of these are, at bottom, common to all persons. They are not be be understood in terms of mere existing preferences but rather as conditions that must be satisfied if one is to live well as a human being; they include physical necessities, personal security, social freedom (from oppressive custom as well as others' interference), and a variety of experiences and opportunities for self-development. To the extent that one is denied or deprived of such conditions, one suffers what Mill counts as "harm."

The question that we face is whether Mill's cooperation examples concern requirements that could not be justified on the basis of preventing harms (on Mill's view or any other), but could only be justified on the ground that they would increase benefits beyond harm prevention. Mill's words imply the contrary. None of his original examples suggest that cooperation requirements may be imposed in order to obtain positive benefits, and his restatement of them later in the essay *On Liberty* implies the opposite. He says that "the fact of living in society renders it indispensable that each should observe a certain line of conduct toward the rest," which includes "each person's bearing his share (to be fixed upon some equitable principle) of the labors and sacrifices incurred for defending the society or its members from injury and molestation" (IV,

3; cf. also IV, 7). This tells us that Mill has in mind preventing harms rather than increasing benefits.

It might be noted that Mill first introduces his examples by saying, ''There are also many positive acts for the benefit of others which he may rightfully be compelled to perform,'' which could suggest that he means ''acts for the positive benefit of others'' and not just acts intended to prevent harm. But this cannot be Mill's real meaning. For under the heading ''positive acts for the benefit of others'' he includes not only cooperation but also Good Samaritan requirements, and these are clearly meant to prevent harm and not to promote further benefits. Mill's words are, after all, transparent: the examples he is introducing concern requirements and thus positive acts rather than prohibitions and omissions.

Let us turn, then, to Mill's talk about ''fair shares.'' His official doctrine is that restrictions on liberty may be imposed only for the purpose of preventing harm to others. He acknowledges that other types of reason might argue against particular restrictions, but he is unclear what they might be. The only examples he provides are these: coercive measures might not be required or might be counterproductive either because the individuals are likely to act better on their own or the intervention would produce as side effects more harm than it would prevent (I, 11). These particular strictures can readily be understood, since Mill is evidently committed not only to harm prevention but also to preserving liberty, interfering with it as little as possible.[9] So, while Mill allows the definite need for some coercive intervention, he wishes to minimize it, as well as to minimize the incidental harm that social intervention entails. None of this commits Mill to considering the fairness of an enforced requirement. Fairness presumably requires that the benefits of harm prevention and the burdens of incidental harm and loss of liberty be distributed in a certain way, according to merit or desert and respecting individual rights. Fairness could conceivably object to some rules predicated upon harm prevention, rules that Mill would otherwise be willing to accept. We can imagine, for example, Mill entertaining the least burdensome rule among a set of equally effective alternatives, that is, the one that prevents a given harm or set of harms at a minimal loss of liberty and a minimal cost in incidental harms. At the same time, we can imagine that such a rule would be condemned by fairness on the

9. See Brown, ''Mill on Liberty and Morality,'' pp. 137–39.

ground that it does not distribute benefits and burdens equitably. Mill's references in his cooperation examples to considerations of fairness would seem, then, to commit him to rejecting such minimally burdensome but effective rules in favor of fairer rules with greater social costs or more extensive limitations on liberty.

Such an abstract, theoretical possibility cannot be denied. But I think the potential problems here might easily be exaggerated. Compare the argument that utilitarianism is defective because it requires that benefits be maximized (and burdens minimized) and thus ignores considerations of justice, which concern their distribution. It is sometimes said, for example, that slavery, which involves the unjust exploitation of some for the sake of others' benefits, might be justified on utilitarian grounds, which shows that utilitarianism is defective. This is, I think, in many ways a highly questionable argument against utilitarianism. But my point just now is that some relevant features of this purely abstract argument against utilitarianism are not available in the cases we must consider with regard to fairness and harm prevention. The principle of liberty permits a "trade-off," but it never sanctions the imposition of burdens on some for the sake of others' positive benefits. No benefits beyond harm prevention can justify coercion under the principle of liberty. The trade-off it allows is loss of liberty (plus some incidental harm by way of side effects or social costs of enforcement) in order to prevent or eliminate greater harm to others. Details of distribution aside, this is a morally respectable position.

The potential problems might be exaggerated in other ways too. An example will help to show this. Mill is concerned specifically with rules that impose requirements such as giving testimony in court or providing some form of public service. Let us take the familiar example of military service, which he suggests. Suppose a society must mobilize a military force in order to defend itself against unwarranted attack. Harm prevention dictates that the mobilization be effective: it must be adequate to secure the community against attack. And it presumably wishes to minimize the harm and loss of liberty that may be required for that purpose. Fairness requires that the burdens be distributed in a certain way. It is worth noting that fairness does not argue, all by itself, for the basic restriction in such a case: it simply sets limits on the means used to achieve other legitimate purposes. It has no objection to minimizing harm and loss of liberty, other things being equal, and it would not require that burdens be imposed when they would not be at all effective in achieving the basic harm prevention project. For simplicity's sake, let us make some assumptions that will not affect the main point of this example. Let us assume that the persons selected by fairness to shoulder the burdens of military service are capable of achieving the harm prevention objective; that the only relevant burdens are military service; that these burdens fall equally heavily upon anyone who shoulders them; that the benefit is security from attack, which all stand to receive; and that all members of the community are equally capable of performing the required service. Now, fairness requires either that these burdens fall on some particular members of the community (because they owe such service to others, let us say, or the others have the right be be excused from service) or it does not. In either case, there are two possibilities: either the class picked out as eligible for military service contains just enough members for that purpose, so that all must serve, or it contains more than enough, so that some might be excused if loss of liberty and other social costs are to be minimized. If the eligible class contains just enough members for the purpose,[10] then there is no conflict between fairness and harm prevention, since fairness does not require any restrictions upon liberty that could not be justified on harm prevention grounds alone. If the class contains more than enough members, then I assume that fairness would not object to minimizing burdens by excusing some in a fair (e.g., random) manner, such as a lottery. In this case, too, then, fairness would not conflict with harm prevention.

I do not mean that there is no difference between the two criteria, that they must inevitably approve of just the same rules for harm prevention. On the contrary, we have been assuming that harm prevention can accept some assignments of burdens that are unfairly made. Suppose, for example, that only a portion of the community is required for military service. Fairness might require that those who have not served before, in such a situation, should be chosen first, while harm prevention would, other things being equal, be indifferent to which members are chosen, so long as enough are mobilized and not too many. This is agreed. My point is, rather, that many arguments from fairness do not require extra burdens, beyond those that could be justified on harm prevention grounds; they require only certain distributions of those burdens. Whenever burdens can be minimized without affecting harm pre-

---

10. In practice, such a calculation must of course incorporate a "safety factor" to provide for unexpected and unpredictable contigencies.

vention efforts, fairness would approve so long as the results are achieved in accordance with some fair procedure. To this extent, arguments from fairness do not function as reasons for imposing restrictions. They accordingly appear compatible with Mill's principle of liberty, which only requires economical harm prevention. And to this degree, at least, it seems reasonable to conclude that cooperation limited by fairness is compatible with the principle of liberty and thus that Mill's examples might present no difficulties for him.

If considerations of fairness are to present a more substantial threat either to Mill's principle or to his examples, there must be cases in which they object, in effect, to minimizing burdens in the course of harm prevention. For, if they do, then they might be regarded as functioning as independent reasons for coercive intervention, and therefore as conflicting with the principle of liberty.

I do not believe that Mill regards them in that way. He discusses justice in *Utilitarianism,* and he says there, ''Justice is a name for certain classes of moral rules which concern the essentials of human well-being more nearly, and are therefore of more absolute obligation, than any other rules for the guidance of life.''[11] Mill plainly believes that injustice and unfairness threaten the most vital of human interests, and that the protection of those interests is the rationale behind the corresponding principles. He thus regards considerations of justice and fairness as rooted in, not as independent of, harm prevention. More important, Mill understands these principles as exerting independent weight in moral reasoning, relative to welfare arguments.

On the usual reading of Mill, he is understood to hold that we are always morally bound to promote the general welfare—that any other way of acting is fundamentally wrong. He acknowledges that we require guidance from some ''secondary'' rules, based on past experience concerning the most reliable ways of promoting welfare. Mill's appeal to considerations of fairness, then, would be understood as an appeal to a particular collection of rules of thumb, rules that specifically concern certain fundamental human interests, but which are to be followed because experience counsels adherence to them, as the best way of promoting welfare. On my reading of Mill, however, this is a caricature of his approach to morality and justice.[12]

---

11. *Utilitarianism,* chap. V, par. 32.
12. I discuss this further in ''Human Rights and the General Welfare'' and in essay 3.

Mill asserts, as a conceptual claim, that morality concerns moral rights and obligations. Moral principles lay down obligations; the principles of justice lay down obligations that correlate with others' personal rights. To be moral is to perform our obligations; to be just is to respect others' rights. To be just, then, one must reject rules that violate others' rights. Mill recognizes no general "obligation" to "maximize utility"; considerations of the general welfare do not enter directly into moral reasoning. Mill believes, of course, that welfare considerations provide the only sound basis for moral principles. But adherence to such principles is not equivalent or reducible to maximizing utility. The principles of justice are predicated on protecting the vital interests of human beings, such as personal security and freedom from others' intervention. They are based on large-scale, long-term arguments about those interests. These arguments yield principles, such as the principle of liberty itself, which lay down rights and obligations that must be respected (save when they are overridden by other moral rights or obligations). In this respect, Mill may be said to "take rights seriously": for they exert independent weight in moral argument; mere welfare arguments cannot override them. Such rights are consequently capable of conflicting with, and overruling, arguments based on harm prevention alone. Equally effective and economical restrictions could be distinguished by Mill on the basis of the principles of justice. If any rules predicated simply upon harm prevention would violate moral rights, they must be rejected. Thus fairness could, in Mill's view, be rooted in harm prevention and still serve, in effect, as an independent condition to be satisfied by morally acceptable restrictions.

Mill's principle of liberty must be understood accordingly. One of the reasons that Mill must recognize as vetoing a harm prevention rule is that it violates moral rights. This reconciles Mill to the idea of accepting rules that impose more than the minimal burdens required for harm prevention alone, if such rules should be entertained. But this qualification on the principle of liberty is itself predicated upon the protection of certain vital human interests, or in other words upon the prevention of harm to others.

Mill's view will not satisfy the critics of utilitarianism who maintain that justice and fairness are independent of utility. They may be right. I have only sketched the sort of view suggested by Mill and described how it might overcome some fundamental obstacles to a utilitarian account of justice. But the adequacy of such an account has no more been established than the contrary.

All of this is, however, beside the point, if we are primarily concerned with Mill's doctrine of liberty. His utilitarian account of justice, while relevant to an understanding of his cooperation examples and the principle of liberty itself, is not entailed by the principle of liberty. Thus, even if one believes that justice is independent of utility, one might wish to consider whether Mill is nonetheless on the right track about liberty and harm to others. For it is not obvious—though it seems often to be assumed—that considerations of justice and fairness, all by themselves, not only help to determine what conduct is right and wrong but also justify measures of coercion. One might question this. One who rejected Mill's account of justice might consistently accept his principle of liberty. One might find reason to agree that considerations of fairness alone never justify coercion, that only harm prevention does.

5

Benevolence and Justice in Mill

Mill regards justice as an important part of morality—perhaps its most important part—but he also acknowledges other moral requirements. Thus, he warns against "merging all morality in justice" by ignoring other moral obligations, such as those of "charity," "generosity," and "beneficence" (*UT* V, 15). Mill provides no general name for the moral obligations that fall outside the realm of justice. His few comments as well as his utilitarianism suggest the term "benevolence"; but we shall find this term misleading, and I shall use instead the neutral expression "nonjustice obligations."

My concern is Mill's division of morality. My aim is to reconstruct for Mill, so far as possible, a coherent set of moral doctrines within the limits of his theories of morality and justice and his version of utilitarianism. Reconstruction is in order partly because Mill does not address the matter directly but also because his views need some sympathetic refinement in the process of interpretation.

Mill's division of morality has not attracted much attention, perhaps because he is usually read as committed to an overriding moral requirement that happiness be maximized, in which case he would seem to have no need or even room for any theory of moral obligation, much less a complex, articulated one. So my first task (which I take up in section I)

Work on this essay was supported by a fellowship from the National Endowment for the Humanities during 1977–78, which I gratefully acknowledge. Earlier versions were presented at the University of British Columbia, the University of California at Davis, and the University of California at San Diego. I am indebted to D. G. Brown, David Copp, Richard Miller, and especially Fred Berger for helpful comments and suggestions.

is to summarize my general understanding of Mill's theory of morality, built around the idea of obligation.

Mill's division of morality has two aspects. One is a *conceptual* distinction between justice and other moral obligations. This concerns the idea of justice and, by implication, the rest of morality, but does not tell us much about the substance of justice or nonjustice obligations. The other aspect is Mill's *substantive* conception of these two general categories of obligation and their requirements on conduct.

Section II takes up Mill's analytic division of morality; section III deals with the substantive doctrines in terms of which Mill views that distinction. Both parts of Mill's theory require interpretation—a choice between two primary readings and a defense of one's choice against both textual and philosophical objections. The initial arguments are presented in sections II and III, but the issues are pursued further in sections IV through VII.

I argue in section II that Mill's analytic division of morality turns basically on the notion of a right. Obligations of justice do, but nonjustice obligations do not, correlate with others' rights, according to Mill, so that an injustice is the violation of another person's right whereas other moral wrongs do not necessarily involve the violation of a right. This is Mill's official doctrine, but not the only way he draws the conceptual distinction. I try to show, on philosophical as well as textual grounds, that it is the better reading of Mill. Nevertheless, in at least one passage, Mill threatens to do the very thing he warns against, namely, "merge all morality in justice" (*UT* V, 15). He does so by seeming to assume, in that passage, that any wrong or immoral act involves the violation of another person's right. This difficulty is discussed at length in section VII. The interpretive hypothesis I finally suggest (with some textual support) is that Mill believes the members of a community generally have a second-order *obligation of reciprocity* towards their fellow members. Although many moral obligations (those falling outside the category of justice) do not *necessarily* correlate with moral rights, when the conditions triggering the obligation of reciprocity are satisfied, an additional, complicating moral factor is introduced into the situation. When one owes it to others to reciprocate their performance of nonjustice (as well as justice) obligations, they also have a right to one's compliance with the same moral principles. So, although rights do not necessarily correlate with nonjustice obligations, rights correlate with the *special* obligation of reciprocity, and these rights are usually at stake when moral principles require us to behave one way rather than another.

I argue in section III that Mill has, in effect, a negative utilitarian conception of moral obligations. Neither the obligations of justice nor nonjustice obligations require us to promote happiness in any direct way. These categories can be substantively distinguished as follows. Justice requires us to *avoid causing harm* to others, while nonjustice obligations require us to go further in protecting others by *helping to prevent harm*. This reading, too, is defended on both textual and philosophical grounds.

The most direct challenge to this reading of Mill is provided by D. G. Brown's significant discussion of Mill's theories of liberty and morality. On Brown's reading of Mill, a wrong act causes harm to others. This leaves no room for nonjustice obligations on the interpretation I propose, which sees them as going beyond harm avoidance to harm prevention. I discuss these matters in sections IV and V, in which I argue, first, that a carefully defined principle of liberty does not generate the difficulty; second, that Mill's analysis of morality in terms of sanctions is better read by emphasizing the internal sanctions, such as guilt feelings and self-reproach, rather than external sanctions; and third, that Mill's views about the enforcement of morality must accordingly be more carefully defined.

In section VI, I try to show why Mill might be inclined to favor a negative utilitarian conception of the basic moral requirements. His apparent argument against paternalism could be extended to yield such a general conclusion, but it could not be so happily contained: pushed to its logical extreme, it undermines Mill's principles of liberty and utility in general. I offer an alternative argument for Mill—one that seems to harmonize with his primary concerns in *On Liberty* as well as *Utilitarianism,* one that emphasizes the importance of autonomy in Mill's conception of human happiness rather than practical difficulties in knowing others' interests. An essential and important part of living well—or living the best sort of life of which a human being is capable, according to Mill—involves finding one's own way, without help or hindrance from others. At this point in the reconstruction of Mill's doctrines, I am to some extent suggesting a revision more than offering a straight interpretation.

In section VIII, I question one aspect of Mill's analytic division of morality—a view that is today, I think, quite widely accepted, though it is not associated with Mill. Although it may be held that any injustice involves the violation of a right, I argue that the converse is not plausible: Not every violation of a right is a matter of injustice. Some moral matters that involve rights are not automatically questions of justice. I suggest accordingly that Mill's division of morality needs refinement. The category of nonjustice obligations becomes even more heterogeneous than it first appeared.

This essay has a further theme—that of reconciling Mill's essays *On Liberty* and *Utilitarianism.* Mill's basic conception of morality is presented in *Utilitarianism,* but that work reveals little about his substantive conception of nonjustice obligations. An important source of clues is *On Liberty,* where Mill suggests the range of moral obligations that he recognizes and offers some comments on morality. His general conceptions of morality in these essays, however, appear to clash. My reconstruction of Mill's doctrines seeks to dispel the inconsistency.

I. Mill's Theory of Morality

Mill is usually understood to hold a moral theory that expresses the most extreme doctrine of benevolence—a theory known lately as act-utilitarianism. This doctrine says that we must always "maximize utility," that is, promote human happiness or welfare as much as it is possible, on a given occasion, to do. On this view, the failure to maximize utility constitutes wrong or immoral conduct. If that is Mill's position, then his talk of "moral obligations" must be taken with a grain of salt. Rules of thumb may be helpful in reminding us of the usual utilities of certain types of action; but a direct application of the general welfare criterion to individual acts is held *always* to take moral precedence. Obligations have no special moral weight.

As I have tried to show in previous papers,[1] however, this reading of

1. See my "Human Rights and the General Welfare" and essays 2 and 3. For alternative readings of Mill, see David Copp, "The Iterated-Utilitarianism of J. S. Mill," in *New Essays on John Stuart Mill and Utilitarianism* [special issue], ed. W. E. Cooper, K. Nielsen, and S. C. Patten, *Canadian Journal of Philosophy Suppl.* 5(1979): 75–98, and works cited there. For a discussion of some of the issues involved in interpreting Mill, see L. W. Sumner, "The Good and the Right," in *New Essays on John Stuart Mill and Utilitarianism* [special issue], ed. W. E. Cooper, K. Nielsen, and S. C. Patten, *Canadian Journal of Philosophy Suppl.* 5(1979): 99–114.

Mill is not the only or the best one. I assume that a moral theory should give special weight to moral obligations (not to speak of moral rights), and I find it possible for Mill to meet this test when one takes him at his word about the nature of morality and utilitarianism. On the one hand, his *principle of utility* says that happiness is the ultimate good, and thus it represents a *theory of value*—not of obligation. As a theory of value, it does not entail any moral requirements, and we are not obliged to understand Mill as making the mistake of assuming that it does—of assuming, in effect, on the act-utilitarian interpretation, that moral requirements are a simple function of instrumental value. On the other hand, Mill appears to hold as a conceptual matter that the rightness and wrongness of conduct is a function of moral duties or obligations, some of which correlate with moral rights. We can understand this so that it does not collapse into act-utilitarianism. Wrong conduct consists in the breach of a moral obligation, that is, a breach that cannot be justified by an overriding obligation. A reconstruction of Mill's view points toward the idea that obligations are determined by the utility of internalized standards of conduct. The principle of utility thus has *only an indirect* role in moral reasoning; it is not itself a moral principle. It provides the basis for evaluating claims about moral obligations (some of which are also claims about moral rights) in the light of the relevant facts. It does not directly determine the rightness and wrongness of acts. Nor is there an obligation to maximize utility, since there is no satisfactory argument to the effect that it would serve the general welfare, in the long run, if we were to internalize an overriding commitment to maximize utility.

The resulting theory of obligation thus diverges from act-utilitarianism and resembles rule-utilitarianism. An important feature of Mill's theory, on my interpretation, however, is that it is based upon his conceptual analysis of moral right and obligation, which tells us how to determine moral rights and obligations by considering the effects of internalized standards of conduct.[2] Mill's ideas about the principles of justice and nonjustice obligations thus assume considerable importance. These principles are the ultimate *moral* guidelines for be-

2. This allows Mill's indirect form of utilitarianism to appear nonarbitrary. Act, rules, etc., have general utility, but the moral concepts tell us, in effect, *how* such values as general utility are relevant to claims of right and obligation and, through them, to judgments of right and wrong conduct. (Mill makes no distinction between duties and obligations.)

havior. They limit the requirements of morality on conduct, and so leave room for supererogation, or meritorious conduct that is not morally required.

II. Mill's Analytic Division of Morality

According to Mill, injustice is a specific type of immorality. It involves "two things: a wrong done, and some assignable person who is wronged." From this Mill seems to infer that "the specific difference between justice and generosity or beneficence" is that, in the former case but not in the latter, there is "a right in some person, correlative to the moral obligation" (*UT* V, 15):

> Justice implies something which it is not only right to do, and wrong not to do, but which some individual can claim from us as his moral right. No one has a moral right to our generosity or beneficence because we are not morally bound to practice those virtues toward any given individual. (*UT* V, 15)

Mill thus distinguishes obligations of justice from other moral obligations in terms of the presence or absence of corresponding rights.

This is Mill's official doctrine—the one he explicitly adopts. But there are two complications here. In the first place, Mill's way of putting the point in the passage quoted tends to run the conceptual and substantive levels of his division of morality together, because he assumes that nonjustice obligations have the content referred to. He assumes, for example, that morality requires us to be generous, which is not a requirement of justice. But it is also clear that his division of morality into justice and nonjustice obligations has two levels—a conceptual level, which is meant to be independent of both utilitarianism and competing doctrines, and a substantive level that, in Mill's case, is of course predicated on service to the general welfare. This is Mill's avowed approach to moral rights and justice. His theory of nonjustice obligations should, presumably, be understood analogously.

We might use one of Mill's examples in a different way to make his conceptual point. As soon as something may be claimed from me by another person as a matter of his moral right, as something that is owed to or due him, my providing it for him cannot be characterized as generosity, since I would only be giving him what is already his. By the same token, someone who appeals to my generosity cannot be understood as standing on or seeking recognition of his moral right to the desired benefit or service; he is not claiming that benefit or service as something that is owed to or due him, as something that is already his by right.

In the second place, Mill entertains a different way of distinguishing between justice and nonjustice obligations—one that is not equivalent to his distinction in terms of rights.

Perfect and Imperfect Obligations

Before Mill settles upon his distinction between justice and nonjustice obligations in terms of the presence or absence of corresponding rights, he observes that the same distinction is sometimes drawn in terms of a contrast between

> duties of perfect and of imperfect obligation; the latter being those in which, though the act is obligatory, the particular occasions of performing it are left to our choice, as in the case of charity or beneficence, which we are indeed bound to practice but not toward any definite person, nor at any prescribed time. (*UT* V, 15).

Mill explains the difference between perfect and imperfect obligations in terms of a tight or loose connection between obligations and the rightness or wrongness of conduct. When a tight connection exists, then the breach of the moral obligation constitutes immoral conduct. (This definition requires qualification—but only qualification—to accommodate the possibility of an overriding moral obligation.) But when there is a loose connection, no such judgment about conduct follows (not even ''prima facie'').

Take the case of charity. Mill appears to assume that one ought to be charitable—one ought to help others by sharing some of one's wealth and resources—but that one is morally free to decide when to ''practice'' that ''virtue.'' If one rarely performs a charitable act, even though one has had ample opportunity to do so, one may be said to lack that virtue, one's moral character may be said to be deficient, and one's *overall* behavior may be criticized accordingly.

But there is a difficulty here. If charity is obligatory only ''imperfectly,'' in the way Mill suggests, then the connection between such an obligation and the morality of conduct is *too* loose for his purposes. For in that case no particular acts of charity are ever required of any person. Moreover, from one's failing to perform a charitable act on a given occasion, when he has the opportunity to do so and no overriding obligation pertains, we *cannot ever* infer that he has breached his moral obligation to be charitable and has acted wrongly. But it does seem possible for someone to act wrongly by breaching a moral obligation without at the same time acting unjustly. Mill apparently wishes to leave room for this possibility. If so, the distinction between justice and nonjustice obligations drawn in terms of perfect and imperfect obligations, as Mill sketches the contrast, will not do.

Consider the idea of a duty to oneself. This is a good example because, though Mill does not believe that we have such duties (that they are *morally* binding; cf. *OL* IV, 7), the idea of a duty to oneself does not seem unintelligible and should be allowed for by an *analysis* of moral obligations or an *analytic* division of morality, such as Mill's. That is done by using Mill's primary account of nonjustice obligations as obligations that lack correlative moral rights. Suppose, for example, that one's duties to oneself prohibit one from commiting suicide or mutilating oneself (except when such conduct can be justified by an overriding obligation). This means that (*ceteris paribus*) one would act wrongly by committing suicide or mutilating oneself. On the distinction between perfect and imperfect obligations as Mill has drawn it, however, this means that a duty to oneself would qualify as a perfect obligation. If Mill drew the distinction between justice and nonjustice obligations in such terms, then, he would be obliged to classify such a duty to oneself as a duty of justice, which is implausible. This consequence is avoided by Mill's official account, that obligations of justice do, whereas other obligations do not, correlate with others' moral rights. For it is implausible to suppose that any person has a moral right that correlates with a duty that he has to himself.

Though Mill expresses dissatisfaction with the terminology of "perfect" and "imperfect" obligation, he does not explicitly reject that way of drawing the distinction. He does not consider the complications I have mentioned. He merely passes on to use the presence or absence of corresponding rights as the basis for his analysis of justice.

But, though Mill does not explicitly reject this second account of the contrast between justice and nonjustice obligations, I propose for the present to ignore it. It would seem unwise to burden Mill, at the outset, with so limited a conception of nonjustice obligations as this second account implies. Later on I shall reopen the question because this way of viewing nonjustice obligations would provide one way of reconciling otherwise clashing aspects of his overall position. But we can postpone these complications until later (see section VII(b)).

III. Mill's Substantive Division of Morality

So far, all we have is a distinction between two types of moral obligations, with no clear notion of what the obligations themselves are supposed to require or allow. Mill tells us very little, especially about nonjustice obligations. Let us consider first what he tells us about justice, and then turn to his examples of moral duties or obligations.

A Preliminary Interpretation

Justice requires the avoidance of harm, and nonjustice obligations require positive benefits. "Justice," Mill says, "is a name for certain classes of moral rules which concern the essentials of human well-being more nearly, and are therefore of more absolute obligation, than any other rules for the guidance of life" (*UT* V, 32). More specifically, "the moralities which protect every individual from being harmed by others, either directly or by being hindered in his freedom of pursuing his own good," are the ones that "primarily . . . compose the obligations of justice." The principles of justice are predicated, in Mill's view, on protecting certain vital interests, such as security; and the chief rules of justice "forbid mankind to hurt one another" (*UT* V, 33).

This suggests a *negative* utilitarian conception of justice, the obligations of which are seen as prohibiting various forms of conduct that harm other persons. Now, since Mill is *some* sort of utilitarian—and thus favors the promotion of human welfare, even if he does not believe that we are always required to act so as to maximize it—it is natural to suppose that his conception of nonjustice obligations complements his conception of justice. Nonjustice obligations may be understood as requiring us to go beyond avoiding harm to others. It is natural to suppose that moral obligations outside of justice require us to act in ways aimed at conferring *positive benefits* and services on other persons, at least to some degree, in some forms, and in some circumstances. If so, "benevolence" would seem a suitable heading for this sector of morality.

Our initial hypothesis, then, is that Mill balances a *positive* utilitarian conception of nonjustice moral obligations against a negative utilitarian conception of justice. Some plausibility is conferred on the positive utilitarian interpretation of Mill's theory of nonjustice obligations by his reference to "charity," "generosity," and "beneficence." Although charity may well be limited to helping individuals in need (and thus might be covered by negative utilitarian considerations), beneficence is traditionally contrasted with "nonmaleficence" and is associated with positively promoting individuals' welfare, beyond mere harm prevention.

In reviewing the texts of *Utilitarianism* and *On Liberty,* however, one finds no reinforcement of this initial hypothesis. Mill offers no further examples of moral duties or obligations (outside of justice) in *Utilitarianism,* and those he gives in *Liberty* seem limited by the aim of harm prevention. We do *not* appear to be morally required, in Mill's view, to confer positive benefits or services on others. The only apparent exception would be when one has undertaken to provide a positive benefit or service for another. But this exception is only apparent, for the case is assimilated by Mill to the obligation to keep one's promises; and Mill believes that this obligation has a *negative* utilitarian rationale.

A Refined Interpretation

Justice requires the avoidance of harm and nonjustice obligations concern harm prevention more generally. In the essay *On Liberty,* Mill offers two sets of examples of moral duties (or what, for Mill, amounts to the same thing viewed from another standpoint: two sets of examples of immoral actions). Both of these suggest a negative utilitarian conception of moral obligation in general. But these examples nevertheless leave room for nonjustice obligations. For Mill can be understood to hold that, whereas obligations of justice are predicated on avoiding harm to others, nonjustice obligations fall within the further reaches of a negative utilitarian conception of morality. Some of the obligations that Mill acknowledges in *Liberty* and classifies under "beneficence" are clearly predicated on preventing harm to others, even when one's failure to perform them could not be characterized as causing harm to others or as failing to avoid harming others. In other words, Mill believes that we are morally bound, not just to avoid harming others, but also to take positive steps to come to others' aid, and more generally to help prevent harm to others.

Mill's first set of examples appear in his initial presentation of the principle of liberty. Mill is concerned throughout the essay *On Liberty* to mark off areas in which coercive intervention cannot be justified. When he first introduces his principle, however, he indicates some cases in which coercive intervention *would* be justified. Some of these examples interest us because they are characterized as cases of moral duty. Thus, Mill says, first, "If anyone does an act hurtful to others, there is a *prima facie* case for punishing him by law or, where legal penalties are not safely applicable, by general disapprobation" (*OL* I, 11). But Mill does not stop there. He says:

> There are also many positive acts for the benefit of others which [one] may rightfully be compelled to perform, such as to give evidence in a court of justice, to bear his fair share in the common defense or in any other joint work necessary to the interest of the society of which he enjoys the protection, and to perform certain acts of individual beneficence, such as saving a fellow creature's life or interposing to protect the defenseless against ill-usage—things which whenever it is obviously a man's duty to do he may rightfully be made responsible to society for not doing. (*OL* I, 11)

One might summarize this passage by saying that Mill believes (a) that we are under obligations to cooperate in some joint undertakings and to act as Good Samaritans, and (b) that these obligations can legitimately be enforced.

One may be tempted to interpret these examples in either of two extreme and contrary ways. On the one hand, one might suppose that some, at least, are predicated by Mill on the idea of promoting welfare rather than preventing harm. On the other hand, one might suppose that they are all conceived of by Mill only as prohibiting us from acting in ways that would cause harm to others. A consideration of these alternative readings will help explain as well as reinforce the interpretation recommended here.

The former way of looking at the examples focuses on Mill's comment that these duties require "positive acts for the benefit of others." Whereas the Good Samaritan requirements, such as "saving a fellow creature's life" and "interposing to protect the defenseless against ill-usage" imply harm prevention rather than the positive promotion of others' welfare, the cooperation requirements might be interpreted in welfare promotion terms. It is commonly held today that we are under obligations of fairness to cooperate in collective ventures, the benefits of which we have accepted, when our turn comes to do our part, where no condition is laid down that these ventures must be limited to harm prevention and cannot be aimed at positively promoting welfare.

Various considerations militate against this first alternative reading. For one thing, it would be strange for Mill to approve of the enforcement of obligations predicated on positively promoting welfare in the context of an essay dedicated to the principle "That the only purpose for which power can be rightfully exercised over any member of a civilized community, against his will, is to prevent harm to others" (*OL* I, 9). If the *enforcement* of such duties can be justified only on harm prevention grounds, then one would imagine that Mill conceives *the duties themselves* as aimed at preventing harms. Furthermore, the harm prevention reading I propose is also compatible with Mill's actual language in the passage. For example, "positive acts for the benefit of others" should not be read as "acts for the *positive benefit* of others": it emphasizes *positive acts,* as opposed to the omission of acts that cause harm to others; and "benefits" often refers merely to the prevention or elimination of harm.

My reading of the examples is also reinforced by Mill's reiteration of them later in the essay, when he summarizes his position by saying that

> everyone who receives the protection of society owes a return for the benefit, and the fact of living in society renders it indispensable that each should be bound to observe a certain line of conduct toward the rest. This conduct consists, first, in not injuring the interests of one another, or rather certain interests which, either by express legal provision or by tacit understanding, ought to be considered as rights; and secondly, in each person's bearing his share (to be fixed on some equitable principle) of the labors and sacrifices incurred for defending the society or its members from injury and molestation. . . . Nor is this all that society may do. The acts of an individual may be hurtful to others or wanting in due consideration for their welfare, without going to the length of violating any of their constituted rights. The offender may then justly be punished by opinion, though not by law. (*OL* IV, 3)

This passage will require further comment later. For now, it should suffice to say that Mill appears to have in mind only the prevention of harm to others as the basis for these requirements.

At the same time, Mill includes within the range of these examples requirements that he himself places under the heading of "individual beneficence"—acts aimed at preventing harm to other individual persons, such as saving lives or defending those threatened with attack.

Although none of his examples suggests that moral obligations require us to confer positive benefits or services on others, they do suggest that nonjustice obligations require us to go beyond merely refraining from harming others by requiring us to take *positive action* (or, at least, to modify our conduct) to prevent harm to others even when, if harm were suffered, it could not be said to have been caused by us.

Thus, in Mill's view, I have a duty to save a drowning man, when I am in a position to do so, even though I may *not* be said to have *caused* the harm he will suffer if I fail to save him (since his plight may be caused by an accident, say, or the action of a third party). Similarly, I am under an obligation to give testimony in court when that is needed, even though my failure to give testimony in many such cases *cannot* be construed as conduct that is harmful or dangerous to others. My being under such an obligation can be explained in negative utilitarian terms— the need for such a rule in the framework of a court system that is ultimately justified on harm prevention grounds. I am under an obligation in such cases, not because I must avoid harming others, but rather because I am required to help *prevent harm,* by giving direct assistance to those I find in need and, somewhat less directly, by cooperating in ventures that prevent harm to others. Lives can be saved and harms to others can be prevented or eliminated by conduct that complies with such obligations.

This brings us to the second alternative way of reading Mill's examples; to conceive of them merely as prohibitions on conduct that causes (or at least threatens to cause) harm to other persons. One may be tempted to interpret them in this way because Mill sometimes suggests that his principle of liberty must be understood quite narrowly, as warranting interference *only* with conduct that causes (or at least threatens to cause) harm to other persons, and these examples are all cases in which coercive intervention can be justified under that principle.

But this interpretation is not compelling. Mill's statement of the principle of liberty does not demand so narrow an interpretation. And the principle, if so narrowly construed, cannot accommodate these very examples—examples that are given by Mill of interference that would be justified under the principle.[3] Mill says, as we have seen, "That the only purpose for which power can be rightfully exercised over any

3. I discuss these examples and their bearing on Mill's principle of liberty more fully in essay 4.

member of a civilized community, against his will, is to prevent harm to others'' (*OL* I, 9). This principle would justify restrictions on conduct that is harmful or dangerous to others; but it can also justify restrictions on conduct that is neither harmful nor dangerous to others, so long as the restrictions are instrumental in preventing harm to others. Mill's Good Samaritan and cooperation requirements (limited to preventing harm) illustrate the possibilities. Mill says not only that we are morally bound to act in such ways, but also that these duties may be enforced. The enforcement of such duties cannot be understood as prohibiting conduct that causes (or threatens) harm to others, but it can be predicated more broadly on the prevention of harm to others. These examples seem to show Mill's belief that harm to others can be prevented, not just by prohibiting or otherwise suppressing harmful and dangerous conduct, but also by requiring or otherwise eliciting conduct that contributes directly or indirectly to the prevention of harm to others.

Mill's second set of examples of moral duties are in line with these in the relevant respect: they suggest that Mill's substantive theory of obligation is predicated broadly on the prevention of harm to others. The second set is offered while Mill is clarifying his approach to ''self-regarding faults''—conduct that is contrary to the interests of the agent but not others. He says that these faults ''are not properly immoralities,'' and he contrasts them with cases that are (and that are thus counted by Mill as breaching moral duties or obligations). Mill's examples of immoralities are these:

> Encroachment on [others'] rights: infliction on them of any loss or damage not justified by [one's] own rights; falsehood or duplicity in dealing with [others]; unfair or ungenerous use of advantages over them; even selfish abstinence from defending them against injury—these are fit objects of moral reprobation and, in grave cases, of moral retribution and punishment. (*OL* IV, 6)

Most of these would be classified by Mill (if he follows his own theory of justice as outlined in *Utilitarianism*) as cases of injustice. But the last example seems to fall under Mill's heading of ''individual beneficence'' (what we are calling Good Samaritan requirements). Mill's use of this example reinforces my interpretation of his substantive theory of non-justice obligations, namely, that it goes beyond requiring us to avoid harming others and requires us to help further in preventing harm to other persons. Moreover, Mill's strategic use of ''even'' at the start of this example implies that he would not go further—that he would not regard as immoral the failure to promote positive benefits for others (save in the performance of voluntary undertakings).

Mill's examples of moral duties and obligations suggest, then, that he conceives of those requirements as predicated on the prevention of harm to others. They go beyond the mere avoidance of harm, and thus beyond the apparent rationale for obligations of justice in Mill's theory, and they extend to the prevention of harm to others; but they do not seem to go any further.

Complications

However, difficulties arise in this reading of Mill—some of them created by Mill himself and springing from apparent inconsistencies among his doctrines. I shall take up the following points:

1. It has been argued that Mill limits wrongful conduct to acts that cause harm to others. We have already considered this claim to some extent, but a fuller discussion of the issue is in order because it points to the connections between Mill's theories of liberty and morality (see section IV).

2. The examples that have guided our interpretation of Mill's substantive theory of moral obligation may appear suspect because they are all cases in which Mill is prepared to endorse the enforcement of morality. One might suppose that Mill believes some moral obligations ought not to be enforced, and it is not implausible to suppose that these would include requirements that go beyond the mere prevention of harm to others. If so, the examples we have considered have been systematically misleading. To deal with this issue, we must consider the relations between liberty and morality in Mill (section V).

3. Mill's views about paternalism suggest one possible basis for limiting moral requirements to the prevention of harm to others. One of Mill's arguments, as given, appears unsound, but can be revised in a promising way (section VI).

4. Some of the difficulties for Mill's theory of nonjustice obligations arise at the analytic rather than the substantive level. In *Liberty* Mill appears to imply that *all* moral obligations correlate with others' moral rights. This would entail that we have no nonjustice obliga-

tions, according to the division of morality laid down in *Utilitarianism*. Several ways of resolving this complication may be advanced: (a) discounting the passage in question; (b) imagining that all nonjustice obligations are modeled by Mill on charity; (c) observing how Mill might find rights linked with some of the obligations that we have assumed he would place outside of justice; (d) taking seriously Mill's suggestion that we are under an obligation of reciprocity to comply with certain useful rules (section VII).

5. In trying to reconstruct Mill's division of morality, however, we should not be guided too rigidly by his conception of justice in *Utilitarianism*. For Mill's analysis of justice is incomplete, and the corresponding category of moral requirements is accordingly too broad (section VIII).

IV. Wrong Conduct and Harm to Others

In an important study of Mill's theories of morality and liberty, D. G. Brown renders Mill's principle of liberty as follows:

> (L) The liberty of action of the individual ought prima facie to be interfered with if and only if his conduct is harmful to others.[4]

Some comment and qualification is required. The idea that is meant to be expressed here is that there is, in Mill's view, *just one good reason* for interfering with someone's liberty—just one reason capable of justifying social intervention—namely, that his conduct is harmful to others. But this reason is not necessarily conclusive, since good reasons can be given against interfering; to capture this qualification, Brown uses "prima facie." As Brown I think would agree, however, we probably should qualify his formulation to read "harmful or dangerous to others," since Mill evidently meant his principle to license interventions against conduct that is dangerous to others, even though it may not be harmful in all cases, such as reckless driving.

Now, Mill's principle of liberty is supposed "to govern absolutely the

4. D. G. Brown, "Mill on Liberty and Morality," *Philosophical Review* 81(1972): 135.

dealings of society with the individual in the way of compulsion and control, whether the means used be physical force in the form of legal penalties or the moral coercion of public opinion'' (*OL* I, 9). From this passage and others it is evident that Mill's principle directly concerns what he calls ''external sanctions'' (*UT* III, 4). A striking fact Brown draws to our attention is that Mill *also* links external sanctions to the idea of wrong conduct. In the same section of *Utilitarianism* in which Mill distinguishes justice from other moral obligations, he traces a connection between ''the idea of penal sanction'' and that of wrong conduct (or the breach of moral obligation). He says, for example, ''We do not call anything wrong unless we mean to imply that a person ought to be punished in some way or other for doing it. . . . Duty is a thing which may be *exacted* from a person, as one exacts a debt'' (*UT* V, 14). Partly on this basis, Brown attributes to Mill a principle of enforcing morality, which he formulates as follows:

> (M) The liberty of action of the individual ought prima facie to be interfered with if and only if his conduct is prima facie morally wrong.[5]

The justification that is referred to here must be qualified as ''prima facie'' because Mill indicates that coercion may not be employed in all circumstances.[6]

Although Brown formulates the principle of enforcing morality (M) similarly to the principle of liberty (L), it must be understood quite differently. For (L) purports to give the *only* good reason for coercive intervention. If (M) were read in a similar way, it too would purport to give the *only* good reason for coercive intervention—but a *different* one; and then the two principles would be inconsistent. Mill makes this clear when he lays down, as a corollary of the principle of liberty, that the wrongness of someone's conduct cannot justify interference (*OL* I, 9).

To avoid needlessly imputing inconsistencies to Mill, without abandoning Brown's main interpretive claim, one must understand the principle of enforcing morality to say (as Brown suggests), not that wrongness itself *gives a reason* for interference, but rather that *there is some reason* for interference when, but only when, conduct is (prima facie)

---

5. Brown, ''Mill on Liberty and Morality,'' p. 148.
6. It is unclear why Brown thinks it is necessary to add the second ''prima facie.''

morally wrong. This allows the principle of liberty to do what Mill explicitly says it does, namely, state the only justification for interference.

If Mill endorsed both (L) and (M), then he would be committed to the proposition that

(P) Conduct is prima facie morally wrong if and only if it is harmful [or dangerous] to others.[7]

This proposition implies that an act cannot be wrong unless it is harmful (or at least dangerous) to some other person.

One reason this result is significant is that it clashes with the usual reading of Mill as an act-utilitarian, according to which he holds that an act is wrong if it simply fails to maximize utility.[8] For one might fail to maximize utility by failing to bring about as much pleasure, joy, happiness, or other positive benefit, either to oneself or to others, as one might have brought about by doing something different under the circumstances, without however harming or endangering another person. So, Mill cannot consistently accept (P) along with act-utilitarianism. More precisely, he cannot accept both these doctrines unless he implausibly believes that one cannot fail to maximize utility without harming or endangering another person; but we have no reason for attributing such a belief to Mill.

Proposition (P) and Mill's Theory of Nonjustice Obligations

For reasons presented in section I, I have no difficulty accepting the idea that Mill is not an act-utilitarian. But I perceive a difficulty for Mill if he accepts proposition (P). For reasons developed in section III, it would appear that his substantive theory of nonjustice obligations rests on the idea that we must sometimes modify our conduct in order to prevent harm to others, even when our unmodified conduct could not be characterized as harmful or dangerous. This would mean that some wrong acts are *neither harmful nor dangerous* to others, but merely fail to help prevent harm to other persons.

7. Brown, "Mill on Liberty and Morality," p. 150.
8. Brown, "Mill on Liberty and Morality," pp. 150–57.

If Mill is not inconsistent, then either Brown's reading or our hypothesis about Mill's substantive theory of nonjustice obligations is mistaken. But if our hypothesis is mistaken, then it would seem that Mill leaves no room in his substantive conception of morality for nonjustice obligations, and it is not clear why he makes a special point of acknowledging them.

The Refinement of (L) and Its Consequences

This particular difficulty disappears if we are guided by my reading of Mill's principle of liberty. Brown formulates that principle as follows:

> (L) The liberty of action of the individual ought prima facie to be interfered with if and only if his conduct is harmful [or dangerous] to others.

But, as I have argued, Mill's principle must be understood more broadly just to accommodate his own examples. This broader reading—which is suggested by Mill's own official formulation—says that interference may be used, not only to suppress conduct harmful or dangerous to other persons, but more generally to prevent harm to persons other than those whose freedom is restricted. Thus, if my freedom is to be restricted, then the justification for that restriction must include the prevention of harm to others.

We might formulate (just for present purposes) the refined principle of liberty as follows:

> (L′) The liberty of action of the individual ought prima facie to be interfered with if and only if interference with it prevents harm to others.

If we conbine this principle with the principle of enforcing morality, then we cannot generate proposition (P). We cannot use it to show that Mill is committed to the view that conduct is prima facie morally wrong if and only if it is harmful (or dangerous) to other persons. We can infer only that

(P′) Conduct is prima facie morally wrong if and only if interference with it prevents harm to others.[9]

Loosely speaking, we might say that the revised correlation of (L′) and
(M) imputes to Mill the proposition that wrong conduct *either* harms
others *or* fails to help prevent harm to others. But this result accords with
our hypothesis about Mill's substantive theory of nonjustice obligations,
which is understood as requiring us to take positive action, or otherwise
to modify our conduct, in order to prevent harm to others, and not just to
avoid harming others.

V. Mill on the Enforcement of Morality

But we must go further. We cannot rest content with the correlation
between the principle of liberty and the principle of enforcing morality
as presented by Brown, not just because the principle of liberty requires
qualification. The correlation may be more radically misconceived. If
so, it cannot be relied on as a guide to Mill's conception of wrong
conduct and, in turn, moral obligation.

The Conceptual Link between Sanctions and Wrong Conduct

So far as the correlation constructed by Brown turns on Mill's analysis
of morality in *Utilitarianism,* it assumes that his theory links the idea of
wrong conduct (and thus of moral obligation) to the idea of *external*
sanctions. For, if it does not, then Mill's analysis of morality does not
generate a principle of enforcing morality, it does not overlap with the
principle of liberty (which is concerned with external sanctions), and it
cannot be used to generate a conclusion about the character of wrong
conduct. I shall argue here that Mill's analysis of morality should be
understood as concerning ''internal'' rather than external sanctions, and
thus that it cannot be used as a basis for interpreting his substantive

9. Some problems arise with this result, as Fred Berger pointed out to me. It suggests,
for example, that an act is (at least prima facie) wrong if it would be prohibited by a
coercive rule that could be justified on grounds of harm prevention—even when there is no
such rule. I do not discuss these complications because I go on to question the correlation
that generates such a consequence. Analogous problems may well accrue, however, to the
reading of Mill that I suggest in essay 2.

theory of morality in the way that Brown suggests. I shall go on to argue, however, that a substantive principle of enforcing morality is revealed within Mill's discussion of liberty.

When Mill traces a connection between "the idea of penal sanction" and the concept of wrong conduct, he clearly stretches the former to cover not just external threats and penalties of an informal, extralegal nature, but even guilt feelings and self-reproach. When he says "We do not call anything wrong unless we mean to imply that a person ought to be punished in some way or other for doing it," he adds, in my view significantly, "if not by law, by the opinion of his fellow creatures; if not by opinion, by the reproaches of his own conscience" (*UT* V, 14). Here "punishment" encompasses self-reproach as well as external sanctions. Furthermore, Mill suggests that self-reproach is not just one among a number of alternative forms of "punishment," the justification of which is connected with the idea of wrong conduct, but rather that it is the minimal, essential sort of "punishment" so linked with the idea of immorality. Mill says that external sanctions may or may not be justified for wrong conduct, but that guilt feelings are always warranted when one acts wrongly.

Brown can accommodate Mill's actual words by qualifying the justification for social intervention that is supposed to be connected with wrong conduct as "prima facie." This allows him to read Mill as saying that external sanctions are not always justified, all things considered, though there is always a presumption in favor of them when conduct is (prima facie) morally wrong.

I do not claim that this reading clashes with the text. I question Brown's reading because it saddles Mill with less plausible contentions than his words, purposes, and conclusions appear to require. One must remember that Mill's enterprise here (*UT* V, 14) is explicitly analytic. He is not laying down substantive principles of punishment, but is trying to display some of the *conceptual* elements of moral obligation and wrong conduct. Mill clearly associates external and internal sanctions very closely, thinking of them all as means of social control and as distinguishable from other devices, such as taxation, by an element of condemnation. But I think we do no favor to Mill if we emphasize his assimilation of internal to external sanctions. Brown's reading represents Mill as extracting from the mere concept of wrong conduct an *analytic* principle of enforcing morality that links wrongness to *external* sanctions; otherwise, the correlation between that principle and the principle of liberty collapses. But the question whether an act is wrong seems logically separate from the question whether others have any warrant for interfering. On my reading, these questions are separate for Mill, whereas on Brown's reading they are not. I understand Mill to claim that wrongness is conceptually connected with justified guilt feelings, but only contingently or synthetically connected with external sanctions. This seems a more plausible position than the one that Brown attributes to Mill.

To see this point, as well as to see some reason to believe that Mill in his considered judgment would prefer my version, consider once again the idea of a duty to oneself. Although Mill rejects the claim that we have such duties, he does not have to be read as maintaining that the *mere idea* of a duty to oneself, requiring one to promote one's own welfare or at least to avoid harming oneself, is unintelligible. He can be understood to hold that ascriptions of such duties are false. They are excluded, not by logic, but by considerations of utility (*OL* IV, 6). Let us combine this idea with another point. Mill holds that others may not interfere with one's purely self-regarding conduct, conduct that would fall within the ambit of a duty to oneself. But he does *not* maintain that the opposite opinion, the acceptance of paternalistic intervention, is unintelligible. I believe that he would furthermore agree that the following position can be held without contradicting oneself: "One has duties to oneself alone, but there is no warrant for interference by others in such matters since they concern oneself alone." If I am right about this—if such a composite claim is not self-contradictory—then the idea that wrongness implies a warrant for others' interference is mistaken; and furthermore Mill would deny such a warrant. If so, we should hesitate to impute the analytic principle of enforcing morality to him when there is room for doubting his acceptance of it.

It follows that we should hesitate to use Brown's correlation of the principle of liberty and the principle of enforcing morality as a basis for understanding Mill's conception of wrong conduct and moral obligation.

This does not mean that Mill rejects "the enforcement of morality." He cannot, of course, consistently with the principle of liberty, maintain that immorality per se is a ground for intervention; but he can believe that the principle of liberty always provides some justification for interfering against wrong conduct. This is because as a matter of fact wrong conduct might have to satisfy a condition that *also* justifies interference under the principle of liberty. Such a position follows from our reading of Mill: conduct is not wrong unless it harms, endangers, or fails to help prevent harm to other persons—which is the condition that warrants intervention under the principle of liberty.

Mill's Principle of Enforcing Morality

Mill seems to endorse a principle of enforcing morality in the essay *On Liberty*. It is not objectionable there, in the way it would be if it were incorporated in his analysis of morality, because it can be understood as a derived, *substantive* principle. The context is Mill's claim that purely "self-regarding faults" do not warrant coercive intervention (*OL* IV, 5–7). Mill makes this claim, however, by contrasting them with "immoralities"—"fit objects of moral reprobation." The latter are "acts injurious to others," including, as we have seen, "even selfish abstinence from defending them against injury." The passage clearly implies that "duties to oneself" are not properly enforceable *because* they are not moral duties or obligations. Mill is not committed to the view that morality per se is enforceable. His position is based on utilitarian reasoning, as is the principle of liberty itself. One is not accountable to others for the performance of one's "duties to oneself," Mill says, "because for none of them is it for the good of mankind that one be held accountable to them" (*OL* IV, 6).

It should be observed that Mill does not regard all moral duties and obligations as legitimately enforceable. When speaking of "acts injurious to others," he says that they "are fit objects of moral reprobation and, *in grave cases, of moral retribution and punishment*" (*OL* IV, 6; emphasis added). This suggests that immoral acts satisfy *a* condition that also must be satisfied by conduct that legitimately may be interfered with, but that they do not automatically satisfy *all* such conditions. They do so only "in grave cases."

Mill leads us to believe, then, that there is a convergence between his substantive theory of moral obligation and his doctrine of liberty. If that is so, then we have no reason to suspect that his examples of moral duties and obligations in the essay *On Liberty* are misleading, just because they are regarded by Mill as properly enforceable. Some moral requirements are properly enforced and others are not, but they are all predicated on the prevention of harm to others.

A New Difficulty

So far, perhaps, so good. But Mill goes further. He contrasts "the loss of consideration which a person may rightly incur by defect of prudence or of personal dignity, and the reprobation which is due him for an offense against the rights of others" (*OL* IV, 7). In context, this statement implies that *all* immoralities are violations of others' rights, which appears to commit Mill to the view that all moral duties and obligations correlate with others' rights. Mill thus seems to make the mistake he warns against in *Utilitarianism:* he "merges all morality in justice" by implying (according to the analysis given there) that all moral obligations are obligations of justice.

This formulation poses a different problem for Mill than the one we have been considering. We have been worrying about the negative utilitarian basis for his substantive theory of obligation. At first this might have seemed to rule out nonjustice obligations; but we have come to see how the prevention of harm to others, when it extends beyond the mere avoidance of harm, leaves room for some limited forms of "beneficence." Now, however, it appears that in *On Liberty* Mill may be excluding at the conceptual level all nonjustice obligations.

We will turn to this matter in a moment. First, I wish to suggest one reason why Mill might wish to place moral obligations within the confines of preventing harm to others.

VI. Paternalism and Benevolence

Mill's rejection of paternalistic intervention (that is, coercive interference aimed at benefiting those whose liberty is restricted) follows formally from the principle of liberty. But this may be misleading. Mill actually offers no general argument for the principle, though he does give arguments for its chief corollaries, such as the rejection of paternalism. One of Mill's arguments against paternalism may be used to explain his rejection of positive benevolence as a moral obligation. But we shall find it unsatisfactory.

The Argument from Ignorance and Risk

Mill's actual argument against paternalism may be summarized as follows (*OL* IV, 4, 12): We know our own interests well, because we naturally care about them; but we do not have reliable knowledge of others' interests, because we do not concern ourselves nearly so much about them. We are likely to be right in judging whether others' actions will adversely affect *us,* and so the use of coercion for the purpose of "self-protection" can, at least in some cases, be justified. But our judgments about the effects of others' actions on *their* own interests are so unreliable as to make paternalistic intervention counterproductive.

One might imagine Mill extending this argument as follows. If we are such poor judges of others' interests, then benevolence is just as pointless as paternalism is counterproductive. To conceive of benevolence as an obligation is to conceive of sound moral requirements that we confer positive benefits on others independently of mutual arrangements. But, given our ignorance of others' interests, any disposition to benefit others is unlikely to be really helpful. It will often be positively harmful. Such internalized dispositions cannot be justified on utilitarianism grounds; so moral obligations are quite properly predicated on, and generally limited to, the prevention of harm.

There are several difficulties with these arguments—both the original one against paternalistic intervention and the suggested extension of it against obligations of positive beneficence. It will suffice, for our purposes, if I show how they conflict with Mill's intentions: the given argument against paternalism is far too sweeping, since its premises would undermine much more than paternalism if they were effective against it.

Mill apparently believes that some coercive intervention can be justified, that is, for the purpose of preventing harm to others. But if paternalism were misconceived because we simply do not have reliable knowledge of others' interests, then we would presumably be ignorant not just of what benefits others but also of what harms them. We would be incapable of usefully directing any sort of coercive intervention. The argument would extend not only against positive benevolence, but also against nonmaleficence: We would have no moral obligations to avoid harming others, either. Indeed, by such reasoning, we would be incapable of making any judgements about the general welfare!

Mill appears to miss these implications of his argument against paternalism because he characterizes the restrictions that would be licensed by the principle of liberty as "self-protection." His metaphor leads him to imagine that we need merely know our own individual interests when evaluating coercive intervention, and need not know others'. But that is a mistake, as Mill himself should recognize. For he often envisages coercive intervention on the model of legislation and its enforcement, and these assume judgments about the interests of persons other than those who initially set the rules or later apply them. Under the principle of liberty, we do not merely restrict persons other than ourselves who threaten to act contrary to our own personal interest. More typically, we restrict persons who threaten to act contrary to someone else's interests. Under Mill's own principle, coercion typcially would be used by one party to protect a second from a third. For such intervention to be well grounded, the first party must have reliable knowledge of the second party's interests.

An Alternative Argument against Paternalism and Positive Beneficence

It does not follow that Mill must reject the idea that we do not know others' interests well enough to act on such knowledge, and consequently must accept paternalistic intervention. An alternative is possible—one that seems implicit in his acceptance of action based on harm prevention, along with his qualms about paternalistic intervention and positive requirements of positive benevolence. Mill can distinguish between our knowledge of what harms persons and other knowledge of their interests. It is clear that he wishes to do this anyway; for his doctrines of liberty and justice both plainly assume that we have knowledge of the vital interests of human beings and of the major harms that one can suffer, and that such knowledge is a sound basis for both private conduct and public action. Furthermore, without some such general knowledge, the principle of utility itself could not be put to any useful work.

Mill believes that certain conditions must be satisfied if one is to have a reasonable chance of living well as a human being. He believes, for example, that we all require certain biological conditions, such as physical nutriment; security in our persons and in others' undertakings to us; freedom from others' interference and from oppressive customs; and even a variety of experiences and of opportunities for self-development. One might suppose that it is the lack or deprivation of such things that Mill chiefly refers to as "harm." The sort of view Mill suggests is that human beings have certain fundamental interests in common; beyond this, they vary a great deal. Because they vary, they have a special interest in being left alone as much as possible, to find their own ways, to develop their own judgment, to experiment with their own lives. Most important, engaging in such activities is an *essential* part of what it is, in Mill's view, for a human being to live well and thus be "happy." In this respect, human happiness cannot be understood in terms of the satisfaction of existing preferences. That is clearly not what Mill has in mind when he discusses happiness most carefully and at length. For, as he well understands, acting on existing preferences and for maximum gratification can be contrary to living well as a human being and thus contrary to one's best, long-term interest (see, e.g., *OL* III and *UT* II, 4–8).

If we understand Mill in this way, we might help him salvage his argument against paternalistic intervention. Since we have reliable knowledge of certain universal, vital human interests, coercive intervention can be predicated on preventing harm, which is constituted by the undermining of these interests. Beyond this, however, coercive intervention is most likely to be counterproductive. This is *partly* because people vary a great deal in their further interests, so that living well will be different for different persons. But living well also involves *finding one's own way*. An added factor, of course, is the clear costs of "compulsion and control." Coercive rules can be justified only when the stakes are comparatively high, the interests to be protected are not speculative but uncontroversial, and the interests themselves do not militate against intervention. Intervention can therefore be justified only when it is predicated on serving a limited range of common, basic interests, or in other words, on preventing the corresponding range of unproblematic harms. To put this another way: Mill suggests an argument for identifying a limited class of "primary goods," the service of which is the only acceptable basis for social intervention. It is not that we lack other interests or cannot be harmed in other ways, but rather that, given a full view of human interests, it appears wisest to limit public policy by reference to these interests and harms.

Such an argument would allow Mill to reject so-called "strong paternalism," which permits interference with others' conduct not only to prevent them from harming themselves but also to make them serve their own positive interests better. This is because Mill would be committed by the foregoing argument to grounding intervention on the prevention of a certain class of primary harms. It follows, however, that Mill may have to accept a "weak" version of paternalism, one that allows interference in order to prevent a person from harming himself, though his version need only be based on protecting those uncontroversial, unproblematic, shared interests, or primary goods.

But this would seem, in turn, a welcome modification of Mill's position on paternalism. For he appears to condemn weak as well as strong paternalism (except in special circumstances), and thus seems to go too far. The idea of a primary good involving the preservation of freedom might show how to account for Mill's obscure condemnation of contracts into slavery (*OL* V, 11). On the revised version of weak paternalism suggested here, Mill can also accept various social schemes that are sometimes urgently needed to prevent harm, even though the beneficiaries might actually reject them, such as mandatory pension plans and medical insurance.

The revision of Mill's approach to paternalism has, of course, another consequence more directly relevant to our purpose here. It suggests how Mill might reject any moral requirements of positive beneficence. His argument would rest in part on variations among individuals and our lack of reliable knowledge of others' interests beyond certain primary goods, as well as the costs of guilt feelings and self-reproach when obligation is put to this additional use. Furthermore, what people need most from us, Mill seems to say, is the secure establishment of certain conditions necessary for a good human life, and beyond that, benevolent tolerance or benign neglect.

We thus have some reason to believe that Mill wishes to limit the range of moral obligations—that he would require us to avoid and help prevent and eliminate harms to others, but would not generally require us to confer positive benefits or services on others. This accords with all the information we can extract from *On Liberty* and *Utilitarianism* about the duties Mill actually recognizes and with the chief doctrines of those works.

VII. Rights and Limited Beneficence

Now we must return to the problem we deferred at the end of section V: Mill's suggestion that all our moral obligations correlate with others' moral rights. This position was suggested in his contrast of self-regarding faults with immoralities, because Mill treated immoralities as violating others' rights. How can this idea be reconciled with Mill's acknowledgment of nonjustice obligations, when the latter are defined as obligations that do *not* correlate with others' rights?

Discounting Liberty

One possibility would be simply to discount the troublesome passage. The only basis that we might have for doing so, I think, is this: *On Liberty* was composed earlier than *Utilitarianism* and does not address itself directly to analytical questions such as those dealt with in the latter work. It seems reasonable to suppose that Mill's concern with identifying the nature of justice led him to appreciate the distinct character of nonjustice obligations and that the analysis of morality in *Utilitarianism* expresses his more considered judgment of these matters.

There may be an element of truth in this way of treating Mill's difficulty, but it is important to observe that alternative accounts are possible.

Nonjustice Obligations as Imperfect

In section II we considered Mill's account of the "imperfect" obligation of charity. Such an obligation is incapable of determining the wrongness of particular actions. If all of the nonjustice obligations that Mill recognizes were like charity, then all wrong actions would be breaches of justice obligations and, accordingly, violations of another's right. This could explain Mill's suggestion that all immoralities violate others' moral rights.

The trouble with this explanation is that it does not account for some of Mill's own examples of nonjustice obligations. Take the case of "individual beneficence," violation of which is instantiated as "selfish abstinence from defending [others] against injury." The latter would seem to count as wrong conduct—and so be unlike the lack of charity—and yet fall outside injustice. One's moral obligation to be a Good Samaritan cannot be modeled on the imperfect obligation of charity, but it does not seem to be (in our or Mill's view) an obligation of justice either.

Perfect Obligations and Rights

Mill's Good Samaritan requirements are not like charity because they do *not* allow free choice about whether or not to confer one's services on potential beneficiaries. When someone is drowning or is under attack and I am in a position to help, Mill believes, I am under a moral obligation to come to that person's aid. If I fail to do so, I may be condemned accordingly, not just as an uncharitable person.

Let us take this further. If I perform only as duty requires, gratitude may be an appropriate response on the part of the person I have helped—but it is the gratitude of someone who also could feel resentment and even indignation at my failing to help him. If he needs my help and I am morally bound to help him, then he may rightfully demand it. He may furthermore assume all those attitudes that one may rightfully hold about another who is on the verge of respecting or failing to respect one's right to another person's assistance. That is to say, in such cases, it is not implausible to suggest that the individuals we are *morally bound to help* may be said to *have a right* to our assistance—not just a right in the weak sense that they would do no wrong in accepting it, but in the much stronger sense that they would individually be *wronged* if denied it. Thus, Mill might hold that one has a right to help from others when the others are in a position to help prevent harm to one in such a situation. This idea would partly account for Mill's suggestion that rights are violated whenever moral obligations are breached. It would, at least, account for Good Samaritan requirements.

It might be objected, however, that this way of reconciling Mill's doctrines in *Utilitarianism* and *On Liberty* is unacceptable, because it requires Mill's category of justice to encompass far too much. All "perfect" obligations, all obligations with a direct bearing on the rightness and wrongness of particular actions, would be included. To avoid this result, one might resist the argument that the beneficiaries of Good Samaritanism be considered as having moral rights to others' help. One might argue, for example, that terms like "moral right" should be limited to cases in which one individual has a certain "limited sovereignty" over another—a claim on the other that he can press or waive at his option, either insisting on the other's performance or releasing the other from the obligation generally or else from its immediate demands. Hart observes that when terms like "right" and "obligation" are limited to such cases, they have distinctive linguistic functions to perform. They are not needed to characterize cases in which one person simply ought or ought not to behave in a certain way and the applicable requirement cannot be waived by the potential beneficiary.[10]

This line of reasoning should not affect our interpretation of Mill's

10. H.L.A. Hart, "Are There Any Natural Rights?" *Philosophical Review* 64(1955): 180–81.

doctrines. In the first place, it is not clear that in the relevant cases the potential beneficiary cannot waive his rights and release the other person from his obligation to help. In the second place, Hart sees "right" and "obligation" as tied together. He would object, for example, not only to the suggested use of "moral right" in Good Samaritan cases, but also to Mill's broad use of "moral obligation" (even when restricted to "perfect" requirements). In the third place, and most important, Hart's strictures are not based on the actual limits of these concepts but amount to recommendations. Hart urges that we refine our use of "right" and "obligation" by reserving them for distinctive purposes. But he recognizes that these terms are not normally so restricted, and thus he cannot claim that Mill's use of "obligation" or the suggested use of "moral right" is conceptually defective. Hart's argument therefore cannot show that Mill would err if he held that all moral duties and obligations that we actually have, including Good Samaritan requirements, correlate with others' moral rights.

However, other difficulties occur with this way of accounting for Mill's claim that all wrong actions violate others' rights. In the first place, one's moral obligation to act as a Good Samaritan does not seem to be an obligation of justice. One trouble with this approach then, is that it tends to overpopulate the category of justice. In the second place, it would render Mill's expressed concern about "merging all morality in justice" misleading, at best, justified only by his recognition of imperfect obligations such as charity. The result would not be satisfying.

It should be observed that Mill's category of justice is already overpopulated, for related reasons. As I shall argue later, Mill is too liberal in classifying obligations under justice merely because they correlate with rights. The category of justice is accordingly too full, independently of Good Samaritan requirements, and must be thinned out by refining Mill's analysis. Before we take on that topic, however, we should consider one last way in which Mill might account for the moral rights that he believes are violated when we act wrongly.

Reciprocity

In both *On Liberty* and *Utilitarianism,* Mill appears to hold that those who benefit in a social setting from protective rules that correspond with principles of moral obligation acquire special debts of obligation to those whose compliance with the rules enables the harm prevention. We

owe it to those others to do our part in supporting these mutually beneficial arrangements.

In *On Liberty,* as we have seen, Mill says that "everyone who receives the protection of society owes a return for the benefit, and the fact
of living in society renders it indispensable that each should be bound to
observe a certain line of conduct toward the rest." One is required, first,
to respect those interests of others "which, either by express legal
provision or by tacit understanding, ought to be considered as rights";
second, to bear one's fair share "of the labors and sacrifices incurred for
defending the society or its members from injury and molestation"; and
third, to refrain from conduct that "may be hurtful to others or wanting
in due consideration of their welfare," even if it does not violate "any of
their constituted rights" (*OL* IV, 3).

Mill thus recognizes *three sets of justified requirements*. He goes
on to imply that these three categories exhaust the sphere of conduct
that is properly subject to coercive social control, just as his earlier
discussion of self-regarding faults implied, as we have seen, that they
also exhaust the realm of ("perfect") moral requirements. The general
picture conveyed here is that of minimal requirements predicated on
the prevention of harm to others, reinforced by considerations of reciprocity:

   i. *Justice.* Some of the rules are described in terms that place them
      under the heading of justice (according to Mill's account in *Utili-
      tarianism*). The first set, for example, protects interests that
      "ought to be considered as rights" (Mill means, presumably, that
      a sound argument is available to support the corresponding as-
      criptions of moral rights). The second and third sets do not in-
      volve rights so directly.
  ii. *Fair shares of burdens.* The second is explicitly concerned with
      harm prevention; rights enter in primarily because Mill requires
      that the burdens be distributed equitably.[11]
 iii. *Individual beneficence.* The third set is likewise concerned with
      harm avoidance and prevention: These are presumably the rules
      under which one is required to aid those in distress.

On the view I am sketching here, Mill would *not* claim that rights
correlate *directly* with the obligations covered by the second and third

11. For a fuller discussion of this point, see essay 4.

categories. This reading therefore clashes with the one suggested under *Perfect Obligations and Rights,* above. Mill presumably holds that one who has indeed "received the protection of society" by virtue of others' compliance with rules in these three categories "owes a return for the benefit" because that protection must have been secured at some cost. The cost is borne by those who have modified their behavior in order to comply with the rules. As a consequence, those others *have a right* to one's compliance in return. Failure to comply with such rules not only harms, endangers, or fails to help prevent harm to others; it also violates others' rights to one's reciprocal performance.

Mill's argument thus resembles recent invocations of the duty of fair play.[12] But note the following points. First, it is limited to require-ments that are predicated on preventing harms to others; it does not go as far as those who invoke fairness in otherwise similar cases to show that one is under an obligation to others for positive benefits. Mill's use of fairness is narrower and presumably less controversial. Second, qualifications can readily be added. Such a right presumably would be forfeited, or perhaps never held, by one who ignores the rules and fails to support them. Third, this line of reasoning obliges Mill to defend a duty of fair play, which presumably must be predicated on the pre-vention of harm to others. I shall not attempt a reconstruction of that here.[13]

Even if Mill is too sanguine about the likelihood of giving such a duty a utilitarian foundation, there seems little doubt that he appeals to it. Somewhat similar ideas are suggested in *Utilitarianism,* for example, where Mill says:

> He who accepts benefits and denies a return of them when needed inflicts a real hurt by disappointing one of the most natural and reasonable of expectations, and one which he must at least tacitly have encouraged, otherwise the benefits would seldom have been incurred. (*UT* V, 34)

Mill's emphasis is different here. He seems to assimilate reciprocity to fidelity, by referring to tacit undertakings that commit one to returning

12. See, e.g., Hart, "Are There Any Natural Rights?" 185–86; and John Rawls, "Justice as Fairness," *Philosophical Review* 67(1958): 179–83.

13. For an account, see Fred R. Berger, "John Stuart Mill on Justice and Fairness," in *New Essays on John Stuart Mill and Utilitarianism* [special issue], ed. W. E. Cooper, K. Nielsen, and S. C. Patten, *Canadian Journal of Philosophy Suppl.* 5(1979): 115–36. Berger's work first led me to appreciate the facet of Mill that I discuss here.

"good for good," rather than fairness. Otherwise, his positions in the two essays seem similar: the benefits in question may be linked to prevention of harm, and the potential beneficiaries can be said to acquire a right to one's help, or compliance, not just as beneficiaries of a moral requirement, but by virtue of one's tacit undertaking to cooperate and comply with such rules in return for the benefits one has received and can expect to continue to receive as a consequence of others' compliance.

In these passages, then, Mill recognizes a *second-order obligation of reciprocity,* incumbent on one who benefits from an effective system of rules predicated on preventing harm to others, which correlates with others' rights to one's compliance, rights belonging to those who have themselves contributed to the harm prevention efforts by complying with the rules.

One special virtue of this line of reasoning is that it promises to restore a distinction between justice and nonjustice obligations. On the account I am suggesting here, not all the obligations that correspond to the three categories of justified requirements themselves correlate with others' rights. Some of them do, such as the obligations aimed at protecting interests that "ought to be considered as rights." But we need not think of the other sets of rules in the same way. When those rules are violated, the corresponding moral obligations are breached, but no rights correlate with them per se. Rather, when such rules exist and one has benefited from others' compliance, a further obligation of reciprocity is established, and others accordingly have a right to one's corresponding compliance.

It seems to me that this last account of Mill's suggestion that all immoralities involve the violation of another's right is to be preferred. It accommodates Mill's clear commitment to an obligation of reciprocity while securing his substantive division of morality. For Mill can hold that obligations to cooperate in harm preventive practices, to act as a Good Samaritan, and otherwise to avoid harming others (even when the harm would not consititute an injustice) fall outside of justice.

On this account, moral phenomena are not simple in such circumstances. But it would undoubtedly be a mistake to imagine that they were. Mill's theory has at least the virtue of reflecting this complexity within morality.

VII. Justice and Rights

I have already suggested that Mill's category of nonjustice obligations breaks down into two significantly different parts, one containing perfect obligations, such as the obligation to cooperate in joint harm prevention efforts and the obligation to act as a Good Samaritan, and the other containing imperfect obligations, such as charity, which do not help determine the rightness or wrongness of particular actions. Now I wish to suggest that Mill's category of justice obligations breaks down too. My main point is that the justice–nonjustice distinction does not correspond, as Mill claims, to the distinction between obligations that do and those that do not correlate with others' moral rights.

Justice

When he surveys the field of justice, Mill finds that it chiefly and most directly concerns (besides rights) matters of desert, impartiality, equality, and voluntary undertakings. By analyzing justice (so far as it affects the rightness and wrongness of conduct) in terms of rights correlative to obligations, Mill claims, in effect, that these other concerns of justice (so far as they affect the rightness and wrongness of conduct) can be analyzed in such terms too.

On the surface, at least, of the matters listed, desert would seem least amenable to analysis in terms of rights. For voluntary undertakings, such as promises, are commonly assumed to create correlative rights and obligations, and it is not implausible to suppose that the relevant considerations of equality and impartiality also can be glossed in such terms. But desert is another matter. For, as Mill recognizes, one can deserve ill as well as good, and the idea of a right to bad treatment appears paradoxical. So, if claims about desert must be translated into claims about rights, it would seem that a simple substitution of "has a right to" for "deserves" will not work. Mill provides no gloss of these other claims in terms of rights, but I believe that we might help him here.

When what is deserved is good, then "has a right to" can do in place of "deserves." When what is deserved is bad treatment, the translation must be indirect. Let us assume that one *ordinarily* has a right to decent treatment by others, under, say, the three types of rules listed by Mill in

Liberty—that questions of desert affecting the rightness and wrongness of conduct arise only in this context. Then we can have recourse to the idea of *forfeiting* one's right to such decent treatment. To deserve bad treatment by others, in view of one's prior bad treatment of them (which is clearly what Mill has in mind), is to forfeit one's antecedent right to certain forms of good treatment by others. If something like this formulation will do, then I think it plausible to say, along with Mill, that all questions of justice concerning right and wrong conduct can be understood in terms of rights and their correlative obligations.

Rights

But, even if this is granted, it does not follow that all questions involving rights and correlative obligations are matters of justice. Mill's general position implies that all violations of rights (all breaches of the corresponding perfect obligations) are injustices. Now, this principle is often assumed; but it strikes me as implausible. In some cases, it seems perfectly natural to say that a person has been wronged and rights violated although no injustice has been done. By this I do not mean that the wrong done or the injury suffered is morally trivial or otherwise unimportant. I mean simply that we would not normally classify some cases as injustices. Rape, torture, cruelty, and unwarranted assault are important wrongs that can, I think, be said to violate the victims' rights, but they would not normally be characterized as injustices.[14] I see no incoherence in refusing to so characterize them, which suggests that the term "justice" is sometimes stretched, rather than applied rigorously, to cover such cases. So Mill appears mistaken in supposing, in effect, that it is analytically true that all violations of rights are injustices.

One might try to save Mill some embarrassment here by invoking Hart's argument against applying terms like "right" and "obligation" to such cases, because they appeal to blanket prohibitions that cannot be waived, as rights can be, by those they are supposed to protect. One may say it is "wrong" to rape, torture, etc., but should not speak of a "duty" or "obligation" not to rape, torture, and so on, or of a corresponding "right." It may be observed, however, that Hart's argument has problematic application to such cases, because willing acceptance of the relevant treatment by the person acted on would (from a moral point

14. Here I follow Hart, *The Concept of Law* (Oxford: Clarendon, 1953) 153–54.

of view at least) remove these cases entirely from such categories (e.g., rape) or would eliminate at least some objections to them, which seems functionally equivalent to the waiving of one's rights. In any case, as I noted before, Hart's linguistic point is more a recommendation than a report of existing logical limits on these terms, so Mill's use of "right" and "obligation" in such cases cannot be excluded as incorrect. Partly for this reason, Mill's overpopulating of the category of justice cannot be avoided or even minimized by correcting his application of "right" and "obligation."

It should also be observed, however, that Mill's problems are not limited to cases in which Hart would prefer us not to use terms like "right" and "obligation." Consider, for example, promises and other voluntary undertakings, which, for the sake of argument, we shall assume give rise to rights and correlative obligations (at least when they may be said to be morally binding). Suppose that I accept an invitation to a party. It then becomes incumbent on me to offer an appropriate excuse if I should fail to attend. How weighty the excuse must be, and whether it should be offered in advance of the event, are matters that depend on further facts about the particular circumstances. Suppose that I know my attendance is important to others who, relying on my word, are reasonably assured they need make no further provision to meet the needs I am to serve. In such a case, we might well say that I would not only breach an obligation but would also violate others' rights should I fail to attend without warning others of my impending absence. But it does not follow, nor does is seem to be true, that I would in such a case do anyone an injustice. In failing to live up to one's word, one wrongs those who rely on it. But infidelity is one thing and injustice appears to be another. Of course, we might have special reason to characterize a broken promise as an injustice—if, say, one not only broke his word but did so to cheat or otherwise take advantage of those to whom one gave it—but such features are not inevitable accompaniments of infidelity. It does not seem incoherent to distinguish between breaking one's word and treating another person unjustly, and it seems to widen arbitrarily the ambit of justice to classify infidelities under injustices.

If my suspicions are sound, then Mill's analytic division of morality (as it concerns the rightness and wrongness of conduct) needs revision because he falls into the trap of linking rights too closely with justice. It may be the case that injustice always involves the violation of a right; but it does not follow, nor does it seem to be true, that all violations of moral rights (even when such violations are unjustified) are injustices. If so, justice cannot be analyzed simply in terms of rights as Mill believes, and issues concerning justice require further differentiation. Mill may be on the right track, but he has not yet gotten to his destination.

This gives us another reason to refrain from placing Mill's nonjustice obligations under the heading of benevolence. Mill needs to refine his theory of justice with the consequence that some obligations correlating with rights will pass into the category of nonjustice obligations. Promising may be useful, but it is hardly a case of benevolence.

Mill's category of nonjustice obligations finally must be a mixed collection of distinctly different moral factors. Then it will more faithfully reflect the complexity of moral phenomena beyond justice.

VIII. Conclusion

I have argued for the following understanding of Mill's theory of morality: Right and wrong are functions of moral rights and obligations. The obligations of justice do, whereas nonjustice obligations do not, correlate with others' rights. Mill believes, furthermore, that obligations of justice require us to avoid acts that cause harm to other persons, whereas nonjustice obligations require us to go further and to act in ways calculated to help prevent harm to others. Mill thus maintains a negative utilitarian conception of our moral obligations.

In the course of the discussion, I suggested how an argument against paternalism that accords with Mill's basic doctrines might be extended to account for this negative utilitarianism. I tried to show how recalcitrant examples could be accounted for once we incorporated within Mill's theory his commitment to an obligation and corresponding right of reciprocity. Finally, I argued, independently of problems that may attach to Mill's utilitarianism, that his analytic division of morality needs refinement, since not every matter concerning moral rights is an issue of justice.

6

Utility and Rights

Two notions concerning the relation of rights to utilitarianism seem widely accepted, by both utilitarians and their critics. The first is that utilitarianism is hostile to the idea of moral rights. The second is that utilitarianism is capable of providing a normative theory about legal and other institutional rights. This chapter chiefly concerns the second thesis, and argues against it. But it also says something about the first. In previous writings I have challenged the first thesis,[1] but here I shall suggest that it is sound. The upshot is that utilitarianism has a great deal of trouble accommodating rights.

This is a revised version of an essay presented to the annual meeting of the American Society for Political and Legal Philosophy on January 4, 1980. An earlier version with a narrower focus, entitled "Utility as a Possible Ground of Rights," was published in *Noûs* 14(1980): 17–28.

In arriving at and revising the views developed in these articles, I have been helped considerably by comments I have received from a number of individuals. These articles developed out of earlier presentations on the subject of utility and rights at the University of Texas, the University of Virginia, Colgate University, and Cornell University. On those occasions I sought to extend the utilitarian account of rights I had earlier extracted from John Stuart Mill's writings. Criticism of Mill's theory of moral rights led me to question the less controversial assumption about legal rights that is principally discussed here. I wish especially to thank John Bennett, Jules Coleman, Stephen Massey, Richard Miller, and Robert Summers for their comments on previous drafts.

1. See my "Human Rights and the General Welfare" and essay 3.

Scope and Plan of the Argument

By "utilitarianism" I mean the theory that the only sound, fundamental basis for normative (or moral) appraisal is the promotion of human welfare. But my argument has implications beyond utilitarianism in this limited sense. It extends in the first place to a number of normative views that are closely associated with utilitarianism but are not equivalent to it, such as normative "economic analysis" in the law. Second, it extends to many other "goal-based" theories and perhaps to other normative theories as well. All of these theories have trouble with legal as well as with moral rights.

Outside ethical theory—in economics and fields that economics has influenced strongly[2]—traditional utilitarian terminology amd doctrines have sometimes been displaced by new ones. To a great extent, this change represents an attempt to secure behavioristic foundations for normative doctrines. Sometimes, utilitarian terms have been given a self-consciously behavioristic interpretation, as when references to "pleasure" and "pain" are replaced by a concern for individuals' "preferences" or one's "willingness to pay." In other cases, normative doctrines have departed from traditional utilitarianism, largely because of worries about "interpersonal comparisons of utility." For example, the utilitarian requirement that the overall net balance of pleasure over pain be maximized has been replaced, in some quarters, by notions of "economic efficiency," some versions of which do not require us (even in principle) to compare the benefits conferred and burdens imposed on one individual with those conferred and imposed on others. The result is a doctrine that is by no means equivalent to traditional utilitarianism. I believe, nevertheless, that my argument applies to these modifications and descendants of utilitarianism. Economists and theorists working in other fields frequently take normative positions that are, for present purposes, similar to those found within the utilitarian tradition. The problems that I discuss in this chapter are, so far as I can see, problems for their theories as much as for utilitarianism.

Later on I shall suggest how these problems beset a much wider class

---

2. See, e.g., Richard A. Posner, "Utilitarianism, Economics, and Legal Theory," *Journal of Legal Studies* 8(1979): 103–40, which also provides references to some of the relevant legal and economic literature.

of theories, including some that are opposed to utilitarianism. These problems concern rights. My argument requires, however, that we distinguish two broad categories of rights, which I shall call "moral rights" and "legal rights."

Some rights are thought to exist independently of social recognition and enforcement. This is what I think we usually mean by "moral rights." These include but are not limited to the rights that are sometimes called "natural" or "human." Natural or human rights are rights we are all said to have (by those who believe we have them) just by virtue of our status as human beings. They are independent of particular circumstances and do not depend on any special conditions. The class of moral rights is broader, since it includes rights that depend on particular circumstances or special conditions, such as promises. Moral rights, in general, do not depend on social recognition or enforcement, as is shown by the fact that they are appealed to even when it is not believed that they are enforced or recognized by law or by prevailing opinion.

Utilitarians are seen as hostile to moral rights; I shall call this the *moral rights exclusion thesis* (*exclusion thesis* for short). Economic theorists who embrace doctrines similar to utilitarianism tend to ignore (rather than reject) the idea of moral rights. Moral rights have little, if anything, to do with normative doctrines of this kind.[3]

Other rights presuppose some sort of social recognition or enforcement, the clearest case being rights conferred by law, including constitutional rights. I restrict my attention here to legal rights within this general class.

---

3. It is sometimes suggested that economic analysis is capable of taking full account of competing normative claims (e.g., claims about justice or moral rights) by treating them as expressions of individuals' preferences (preferences frustrated when institutions would be regarded by such individuals as violating moral rights or breaching other moral principles). See, e.g., Guido Calabresi and A. Douglas Melamed, "Property Rules, Liability Rules, and Inalienability: One View of the Cathedral," *Harvard Law Review* 85(1972): 1089–1128. But this is inadequate. Someone who claims, for example, that slavery is morally unacceptable because it violates basic human rights may be expressing a preference against slavery, but he is doing more than that. He is claiming in this context that (P) considerations of efficiency alone could not justify slavery. The question to be faced is not whether slavery will frustrate preferences but whether claim (P) is true. To understand this as a question about preferences (even enlarging it to include the preferences of people other than those who embrace the claim) is to look at these matters from the standpoint of economic analysis and thus to beg the very question at issue, namely, whether economically efficient institutions can be morally unacceptable because they violate rights.

It is generally assumed that utilitarians have no difficulty accommodating legal rights and providing a normative theory about them; I shall call this the *legal rights inclusion thesis* (*inclusion thesis* for short). Normative theorists working within economics and policy studies are concerned with telling us which legal rights should be conferred, and take for granted that their theories are capable of accommodating such rights. I shall argue that they are mistaken.[4]

The main part of my argument may be summarized as follows. The exclusion thesis assumes that moral rights make a difference to evaluation of conduct by excluding a range of direct utilitarian arguments that might militate against conduct (but not when it involves the exercise of rights) or that might justify conduct (but not when it would interfere with the exercise of rights). I call this the *moral force,* or *normative force* of moral rights. The inclusion thesis assumes, by contrast, that legal rights are morally neutral and do not automatically possess normative force. But, when legal rights are regarded as justifiable or morally defensible, they are regarded as having moral force. In other words, the idea that legal rights are morally defensible entails the idea of a moral presumption in favor of respecting them (even though it may not be useful to exercise them or it may be useful to interfere with them in particular cases). The problem for utilitarianism, then, is whether it can somehow accommodate the moral force of justified legal rights. I argue that it cannot do so satisfactorily. Although there are often utilitarian reasons for respecting justified legal rights, these reasons are not equivalent to the moral force of such rights, because they do not exclude direct utilitarian arguments against exercising such rights or for interfering with them. Specifically, utilitarian arguments for institutional design (the arguments that utilitarians might use in favor of establishing or maintaining certain legal rights) do not logically or morally exclude direct utilitarian arguments concerning the exercise of, or interference with,

4. It is sometimes suggested that when we speak of "moral" rights we are referring to rights that ought to be conferred amd enforced by social institutions. On this view, a utilitarian's normative theory of institutional rights is equivalent to a theory of moral rights. This notion does not affect the present argument. I believe it, however, to be mistaken. To say that rights ought to be respected is not to imply that they ought to be enforced, even by extralegal institutions. Respect for rights can simply amount to doing what the corresponding obligations require, and from the fact that one is under an obligation (even an obligation correlative with another person's rights), it does not follow that any sort of coercion, strictly speaking, is justified for the purpose of ensuring obligatory performance or penalizing nonperformance.

such rights. As a consequence, evaluation of conduct from a utilitarian standpoint is dominated by direct utilitarian arguments and therefore ignores the moral force of justified legal rights. The utilitarian is committed to ignoring the moral force of those very rights that he is committed to regarding as having moral force by virtue of the fact that he regards them as morally justifiable.

Bentham's Approach

Of the classical utilitarians, Bentham is the one whose approach is most directly analogous to that of contemporary economic theorists as well as to that of utilitarians who wish to provide a normative theory of legal rights. He accepted the exclusion and inclusion theses. And so it is useful to begin with his ideas.

We are often reminded that Bentham dismissed the very idea of natural rights as "nonsense." One reason, of course, was his rejection of certain doctrines associated with natural rights, such as the notion that they are conferred by nature or discovered by the pure light of natural reason. But Bentham in effect rejected moral rights generally, that is, rights that do not presuppose social recognition or enforcement.[5]

Bentham's most direct, official reason for rejecting moral rights derives from his analysis of statements about rights and obligations. He held that meaningful statements about rights must be understood as statements about beneficial obligations, and he held that statements about obligations concern the requirements of coercive legal rules. He held that one has a right if and only if one is supposed to benefit from another person's compliance with a coercive legal rule. It follows that he could not recognize rights that are independent of social recognition or enforcement, that is, moral rights.

These analytical doctrines have no straightforward relation to Bentham's utilitarianism. His analysis of rights neither follows from a principle of utility nor entails it. Nevertheless, it is arguable that, given his utilitarianism, Bentham could not have accepted the idea that we have

5. For Bentham's analysis of rights, see essay 1 and Hart, "Bentham on Legal Rights," in *Oxford Essays in Jurisprudence: Second Series,* ed. A. W. B. Simpson, pp. 171–201 (Oxford: Clarendon, 1973). Bentham did accept the idea of "natural liberties" but only in the sense that one is "free" to do whatever is not restricted by coercive social rules.

any moral rights. It would seem that his utilitarianism commited him to the exclusion thesis.

One might argue for the incompatibility of utilitarianism and moral rights as follows. Moral rights are not merely *independent of* social recognition and enforcement but also provide *grounds for appraising* law and other social institutions. If social arrangements violate moral rights, they can be criticized accordingly. Moral rights call for the establishment of institutions that respect them. But Bentham held that institutions are to be evaluated *solely* in terms of human welfare. Unless we assume that arguments based on moral rights converge perfectly with those based on welfare, it would seem that a utilitarian like Bentham would be obliged to reject moral rights.

This reasoning appears, however, to assume rather than prove the exclusion thesis. Why should we suppose that arguments based on moral rights diverge from welfare considerations? The answer has to do with the normative character of rights. If I have a right to do something, this provides *an argumentative threshold* against objections to my doing it, as well as a presumption against others' interference. Considerations that might otherwise be sufficient against my so acting, in the absence of my having the right, or that might justify others' interference, are ineffective in its presence.

Consider, for example, the idea that I have a right to life. This entails that I may act so as to save it and that others may not interfere, even if these acts or the results would otherwise be subject to sound criticism. I need not show that my life is valuable or useful, and the fact that my defending it would have bad overall consequences or is otherwise objectionable does not show that my defending it is wrong, or that others' interference is not wrong. My right provides a measure of justification for certain actions of my own, as well as limits to interference. I call this argumentative threshold character the moral force of moral rights.

This point is sometimes distorted by exaggeration. Note, however, that my right to life does not automatically justify any course of action whatsoever that may be needed to save it; nor does it absolutely block justification for others' taking my life. Rights are not necessarily "absolute." That is why I speak of thresholds that need to be surmounted.[6]

6. The sort of exaggeration cautioned against here is unfortunately suggested by Ronald Dworkin's speaking of rights as "trumps" against utilitarian arguments. See the title essay of his *Taking Rights Seriously* (Cambridge: Harvard University Press, 1978). But as Dworkin makes clear, he does not assume that rights are generally "absolute" (see, e.g., pp. 191–92).

Let us apply this to utilitarianism. From the standpoint of this theory considerations of welfare are morally relevant in the following way. The fact that an act would promote welfare to a greater degree than would the alternatives (no matter how small the difference) provides sound reason to prefer that course of action. However, the mere prospect of increasing welfare to some degree (however slight) is incapable of surmounting the argumentative threshold of my rights. I may defend my life even at *some* cost to overall welfare, and others may not interfere *just* because it would promote overall welfare to *some* degree if they did. In this way, the arguments that flow from moral rights appear to diverge from those predicated on the service of welfare. If one accepts moral rights, one cannot accept absolute guidance by welfare arguments. And so we have the moral rights exclusion thesis.

Similar considerations apply to normative doctrines in economics and other fields that are developed in terms like ''economic efficiency.'' If one believes that institutions are to be evaluated solely in terms of their promotion of such values, and not in terms of independent rights, one cannot accept the idea that we have any moral rights.

Bentham's attitude toward legal rights was of course different. His analysis of rights in terms of the beneficial requirements of coercive legal rules allows for the possibility of legal rights. And the general idea that utilitarianism is compatible with legal rights is hardly controversial, being widely assumed in law, economics, and political theory. Much the same idea is presupposed by what is called ''the economic analysis of law'' (though only the normative versions of ''economic analysis'' interest us here).

The legal rights inclusion thesis assumes that institutions serving the general welfare or economic efficiency are capable of conferring rights. Critics of utilitarianism as well as critics of normative economic analysis (including those who believe we have moral rights) do not challenge this

---

My suggestion that rights have normative or moral force derives from Dworkin's discussion but differs from it in several ways: (1) I distinguish moral from legal rights and attribute moral force to legal rights only when they are defensible or justified. (2) The normative force of rights cannot be understood simply in terms of their relation to utilitarian arguments (as Dworkin originally suggested) but must be considered more generally; my discussion attempts to allow that. (3) Dworkin's distinction between ''strong'' and ''weak'' rights corresponds roughly to the two aspects of normative force in my discussion: ''strong'' rights provide obstacles to the justification of others' interference, while ''weak'' rights provide justifications for one's own behavior. Dworkin's argument seems to rely on both aspects of the normative force of rights.

assumption. They may claim that utilitarian or economically efficient institutions would establish some rights that ought not to be established (such as certain property rights) or would violate some rights that ought to be respected (such as rights to privacy or to personal autonomy), but they do not claim that such institutions are incapable of conferring any rights at all.

This is a plausible assumption, at least when it is coupled with a morally neutral conception of legal rights, by which I mean a conception that generates no moral presumption that those rights should be respected. Furthermore, the idea that utilitarian and efficient institutions confer rights leaves plenty of room for opponents of utilitarianism and of normative economic analysis to criticize those institutions, on the basis of moral rights or other values.

I am sympathetic to the morally neutral conception of legal rights, for reasons such as the following. The law of a society may be understood as implying that people have certain rights. But the law may be outrageously unjust, and hence the rights it confers may be morally indefensible. For example, there is no moral presumption favoring respect for the legal rights conferred by chattel slavery. Circumstances may of course provide some reasons for respecting morally objectionable entitlements. Those on whom such rights may be conferred are, after all, human beings who can claim some measure of respect and consideration from others too. But, while these considerations may affect what we ought to do in the context of morally outrageous institutions, they do not show anything about the moral force of legal rights themselves. So I am prepared to say that, from the fact that I have a right conferred on me by law, *nothing follows* concerning what I or others may rightfully do. We might put this point by saying that *merely legal rights have no moral force.*[7]

If I am wrong about legal rights in this respect, then all have moral force. If we could assume that, my argument would be simpler. Since I deny it, I must limit my attention to those legal rights with moral force. These are legal rights that are taken to be morally defensible, the rights conferred by laws that are supposed to be justified. Let us see what this amounts to.

7. Dworkin sometimes appears to assume that all legal rights have moral force; see *Taking Rights Seriously,* pp. 326–27. He cancels this suggestion in "'Natural' Law Revisited," *University of Florida Law Review* 34(1982): 183–87 and in *Law's Empire* (Cambridge, Mass.: Harvard University Press, 1986), pp. 101–12.

Legal Rights with Moral Force

Suppose that Mary rents a house that comes with a garage for her car. Access to the garage is provided by a private driveway, which she alone is authorized to use. Sometimes, however, she finds someone else's car parked in the driveway, which prevents her from parking or leaving with her own car. This may be inconvenient or it may not. Whenever it happens, however, Mary's rights are not being respected by other individuals.

Mary's rights depend on social arrangements, and they are enforceable by legal means. They thus qualify as legal rights. I shall assume, however, that these rights are *not merely* legal. I am supposing, in other words, that the social arrangements presupposed by Mary's rights and their enforceability are justifiable; those institutions or their relevant parts are morally defensible. This does not seem an implausible assumption to adopt. From the fact that Mary's rights are not shared by others, for example, we cannot infer that they are morally objectionable. I would suppose that ordinary rights like Mary's can arise and be justified in otherwise unjust as well as just societies, though this is not required for the argument. Within a society in which people have fair shares of the resources and considerable freedom to decide how to use their respective shares, for example, some individuals, with needs that are different from Mary's, may reasonably decide to make arrangements that are different from hers. And in such a society there may be good reason to have rights like Mary's made enforceable by law. Of course, Mary's rights are meant only as an example. If one has objections to private parking arrangements, it should be possible to substitute another example for the purpose. It is useful, however, to choose *very ordinary* rights, which clearly depend on institutional arrangements and legal recognition or enforcement. What I think we can agree about Mary's rights applies to many other routine legal rights, that is, to rights we assume are morally defensible.

Given the arrangements that Mary has made, she may use the garage and driveway as she wishes. She may permit others to use them or refuse to do so. Others may not use them without her permission. In other words, Mary's rights make a difference to what she and others may justifiably do.

The principal assumption I shall make is this: when we regard Mary's rights as morally defensible, on any basis whatsoever, we also regard them as having moral force. The differences that her rights make to the evaluation of conduct obtain, not just in the eyes of the law, but also from a moral point of view. We may disagree about the conditions that must be satisfied if legal rights are to be morally defensible. But, if we hold that Mary's rights are morally defensible, then we are committed to agreeing that they have such force. Utilitarians and nonutilitarians will disagree about the conditions that justify legal rights. This is compatible, however, with their agreeing that certain legal rights are morally defensible. And the latter entails, as I shall assume, that such rights have moral force. To deny that Mary's legal rights have such force is to deny that they are morally defensible.

Mary's rights make a difference even when they are infringed. If others encroach upon her rights thoughtlessly or for their own private convenience, for example, it is incumbent on them to apologize or even, perhaps, to compensate her for any inconvenience she has suffered as a consequence. If they fail to do so, then that is a reason for judging them to have acted wrongly. If compensation should be offered, then Mary is free to accept it or refuse it, as she prefers.

Of course, Mary's rights are limited. The driver of an emergency vehicle on an urgent errand might justifiably block Mary's driveway without first obtaining Mary's permission—even, perhaps, in the face of her refusal to give permission. This holds from a legal as well as a moral standpoint. And, to simplify matters here, I shall assume that the legal limits of Mary's rights correspond perfectly to what we should regard on reflection as their proper limits from a moral point of view. Limits like these on Mary's rights are compatible with the idea that her rights make a difference to moral arguments. We need not assume that Mary's rights are "absolute" and overwhelm all conflicting considerations. My point is simply that Mary's rights entail an argumentative or justificatory threshold. Certain considerations are capable of justifying encroachments on Mary's rights, but not all are. Let us look at this more closely.

If one regards Mary's moral position from a utilitarian standpoint, then one might be presumed to reason as follows. Mary is fully justified in exercising her legal rights only when and as she can promote human welfare to the maximum degree possible, and others are fully justified in encroaching on Mary's rights in the same sort of circumstances and for the same sort of reason.

This reasoning may be framed in probabilistic terms. What may be thought required, then, is not that human welfare actually be promoted to the maximum degree possible, but that Mary's acts, when she exercises her rights, or the acts of those who encroach on them, be *most likely* to maximize human welfare (or something of the sort). This type of qualification will not, I think, affect the present argument, and I shall generally ignore it hereafter.

The utilitarian pattern of reasoning that I have sketched seems to clash with the idea that Mary's rights are morally defensible and thus have moral force. For it assumes that Mary's rights *make no difference* to what she and others may justifiably do, except insofar as the legal recognition of those rights changes circumstances so that certain possible courses of action have added utility or disutility. But this is not the way Mary's moral position is ordinarily viewed when it is assumed that her legal rights are morally defensible.

Suppose, for example, that a neighbor decides late at night to park his car in Mary's driveway, without obtaining her permission, in order to save himself a long cold walk from the nearest legal parking space. He might reason soundly that Mary is unlikely to be inconvenienced, since he shall move his car early the next morning. And that might turn out to be the case. Nevertheless, Mary might justifiably resent and complain of his presumption. Of course, Mary could reflect that she might have been seriously inconvenienced if an emergency had arisen during the night and she was unable to use her car. But it should not be assumed that her resentment would be justified solely by the possible inconvenience she might have suffered. For that might have happened even if she had given permission beforehand for him to use the driveway, in which case her resentment would not be warranted. Her belief is that her neighbor acted unjustifiably—that his action could not be justified simply by calculations of actual or probable utilities.

We can generalize these points as follows. Mary has the moral freedom to exercise her rights, within certain limits. Neither this freedom nor its limits can be explained by the utilitarian line of reasoning we have described. For example, Mary may act to her own disadvantage, without the prospect of compensating advantages to anyone else. Her rights also permit her some indifference to the effects of her choices upon others. They permit her, for example, to inconvenience others while exercising her rights, without the prospect of compensating advantages to anyone, including herself. She need not act so as to maximize utility when she exercises her rights. Similarly, others may not act in certain ways without her permission, even if their doing so would maximize utility.

A utilitarian might object that he is not interested in Mary's rights as such but only in evaluation of her conduct and that of others. He might suggest that I have ignored the distinction between Mary's having rights and the conditions under which she justifiably exercises them. But I have framed my argument so as to respect that distinction. My point is not that Mary's rights completely determine what she and others may justifiably do but that her rights make a difference to the evaluation of her and others' conduct, a difference that unrestricted utilitarian reasoning cannot accept. The difference is not simple, since we cannot assume that Mary's rights are "absolute." In the present context, the difference amounts to this: from the mere fact that net utility would not be maximized by her exercising her rights, we cannot infer that her exercise of them is not justified; similarly, from the mere fact that net utility would be maximized by encroaching on her rights, we cannot infer that one is justified in encroaching on them.

One thing that complicates matters here is that Mary's rights, to be morally defensible, must have some foundation in human interests, needs, or welfare and are limited in turn by similar considerations. For this reason, utilitarian considerations are, *within limits,* relevant to a final determination of what Mary and others may justifiably do, which is bounded by a decent regard for others' welfare. Mary's decisions must give some respect to the interests of others, and what others may justifiably do is determined in part by the effects of their conduct upon people generally. Thus, despite her rights, Mary may not deny access to her driveway to someone in dire need, and others may use it without her permission if the need is pressing. But this is not to say that utilitarian reasoning *generally* determines how Mary and others may justifiably act. Let us suppose that *very substantial* utilities or disutilities outweigh the moral force of Mary's rights. We cannot infer from this that *minimal increments* of utility are sufficient to outweigh those arguments. To reason in that way would assume that Mary's rights make no difference to moral argument or, in other words, that her rights lack moral force. But, if I am right, Mary's legal rights have moral force if they are morally defensible.

It should be emphasized that I am assuming there is no moral objection to Mary's having such special control over her garage and driveway. I do not mean to suggest (and I have explicitly denied) that any arbitrary arrangements that Mary might secure under the law would have similar moral consequences. I would not suggest, for example, that if the law gave Mary comparable control over another human being—if, in other words, it regarded her as the owner of a chattel slave—then she would be morally free to decide, in a similar way, how to use that person. Even if the law regarded Mary in that way, we might reasonably deny that the legal arrangements make any difference to the way that Mary may justifiably behave, from a moral point of view. But our example is not like that. I have deliberately chosen to focus on an ordinary, mundane legal right that might plausibly be regarded as morally defensible.

It is also important to emphasize that I have not been discussing moral rights, that is, rights we are supposed to have independently of social recognition or enforcement. Nor is it suggested that Mary's rights arise of their own accord, without any foundation in fact. What is suggested, rather, is that, given the relevant facts in the social circumstances, which have to do with Mary's unobjectionably renting a house with a garage serviced by a driveway, she assumes a new moral position. She acquires rights, and her acquired rights appear to function as more or less stable moral factors with characteristic implications.

I have not claimed that there can be no utilitarian foundation for Mary's rights. It might be argued, for example, that the general welfare can be served by institutional arrangements that provide Mary with such special control over her garage and driveway. Let us now see how this argument would proceed, and what it might prove.

Utilitarian Institutions

Although Bentham is widely thought to be committed to the pattern of utilitarian reasoning I have been discussing, he does not seem to deal with problems of the sort we have considered. Bentham and those who follow in his footsteps, including those wedded to normative economic analysis, are concerned with the evaluation of law and social institutions. In this connection, Bentham applies the standard of utility, not to individual acts taken separately, but rather to the rules and institutions that he thinks of as conferring rights. Those favoring economic analysis use a standard of efficiency in a similar way. They criticize, evaluate, and recommend legal rules in terms of some value that the rules are supposed to serve. These theorists assume, in accordance with the inclusion thesis, that rights would be conferred by institutions they regard as justified.

It does seem plausible to suppose that institutions conforming to utilitarian requirements or to the dictates of economic efficiency would incorporate rights. In the first place, when we consider possible institutions, we naturally tend to model them on those with which we are familiar, and these are generally assumed to confer rights. In the second place, and most importantly for present purposes, it seems reasonable to suppose that institutions designed to serve the general welfare or economic efficiency are capable of satisfying a *necessary* condition for incorporating rights. That is, the rules of such institutions might confer the proper range of freedom and impose the appropriate restrictions upon others' behavior that correspond to rights like Mary's. I know of no general argument that could deny this possibility.

When Bentham assumed that rights would be incorporated in utilitarian institutions, he proceeded on the assumption that rights exist whenever coercive restrictions upon behavior serve the interests of determinate individuals. It is difficult to imagine how institutions supported by the best utilitarian arguments could fail to create some useful restrictions, and it is natural to suppose that some of these restrictions would be useful by serving or securing the interests of specific persons. So, on Bentham's theory, it would seem that such institutions confer rights.

Economic theorists have not devoted much attention to the question of what it is to have a right. But it is reasonable to suppose that they have been guided by some conception of rights like Bentham's.

But we cannot pursue the basic issue here within the framework constructed by Bentham. Our question is not whether rights as Bentham conceived of them can be reconciled to utilitarianism, nor whether rights as economic analysts conceive of them can be reconciled with the principles of economic efficiency. This is so for two distinct reasons.

In the first place, it could be said that Bentham took rights a bit too seriously. He inflated their normative force into coercive power. He imagined that, when I have a right, existing legal rules provide for their enforcement. But enforcement is not an essential feature of rights, even legal rights. Rights can be recognized by law even when no legal provisions are made for their enforcement. Consider, for example, those civil rights of U.S. citizens that are based upon the "equal protection clause" of the Constitution. These rights went without enforcement for many years. The Civil Rights Acts and the Civil Rights Division of the U.S. Department of Justice were intended as means for securing these rights. Enforcement enhances these rights and establishes new "secondary" rights, but it does not create the basic constitutional rights themselves. Legal rights are not necessarily enforced, and their enforcement need not even be authorized. It follows that neither enforcement nor its authorization is an essential feature of legal rights. Bentham was mistaken. In consequence, at least part of the reason theorists sometimes think they have for concentrating upon legal rights while ignoring moral rights is an illusion.

In the second place, Bentham's analysis ignores the moral force of rights under justified institutions. The question that we face is whether utilitarianism or comparable theories can accommodate legal rights with moral force.

This qualification is important, and it does not prejudice our inquiry in any way that is unfair to utilitarianism or normative economic analysis. The institutions that a utilitarian or an economic analyst regards as fully justified are, presumably, his best candidates for institutions that create rights with moral force. If such a theorist regards some institutions as *justified* but he *cannot* accommodate the moral force of legal rights conferred by those institutions, then his theory is in trouble, faced with a kind of incoherence. On the one hand, he wishes to claim that the institutions he can justify would confer some rights. On the other hand, his basic theory does not allow him to accommodate the moral force possessed by legal rights in justified or morally defensible institutions. This is what I shall now try to show.

The Relevance of Direct Utilitarian Arguments

The strategy of my argument is as follows. I shall suppose that a utilitarian or economic analyst believes that certain rights would be conferred by legal institutions that are justified by his basic normative principles. I take this to imply that the rights are to be regarded as morally defensible and thus that we can consider them as having moral force. I shall then try to show that this force cannot be accommodated by a normative position developed on the foundation of welfare or some comparable value such as economic efficiency.

For purposes of illustration, let us suppose that a utilitarian or economist believes that we can justify a set of institutions like those assumed in our example. Under the rules of those institutions, Mary has exclusive use of the garage and driveway attached to the house she is renting (though others' use of them is permitted under special circumstances, even without her permission). We shall assume, furthermore, that the freedom conferred on Mary by the rules and the obligations imposed by them on other persons match precisely what we should regard on reflection as the proper extent and limits of her rights when viewed from a moral standpoint. Mary is not required to worry generally about the utility of her actions or about economic efficiency when deciding how to use her garage or driveway or whether to permit others to use them. Nor are others expected to decide whether to use Mary's garage or driveway just on the basis of the utility of such conduct or its efficiency. And officials are not expected to decide on such grounds when they are called upon to apply or enforce the relevant and clear legal rules.

Unless something like this can be assumed, the idea that legal rights with moral force can be accommodated by a theory based on welfare or efficiency is defeated at the start. But the assumption appears reasonable. At least, I know of no general argument that could deny the possibility that such institutions as would be preferred by a utilitarian or by an economist might confer the proper ranges of freedom and the appropriate restrictions on others' behavior that correspond to the moral force of ordinary legal rights like Mary's. It should be emphasized, of course, that we are not supposing that such institutions would respect all rights that ought to be respected, including moral rights, which are independent of social recognition and enforcement, or that such institutions satisfy any other normative standards that a critic of utilitarianism or of normative economic analysis may endorse. These are concerns that a utilitarian or an economic analyst cannot be thought to share. Our strategy is to accept the normative approach of utilitarians and of economic analysts and to see where that leads us.

It must also be emphasized, however, that these assumptions do not settle the present issue. They imply only that such theories are capable of satisfying a *necessary* condition for accommodating legal rights with moral force. But our question is not whether utilitarianism or efficiency analysis could regard such institutions as justified or morally defensible. Our question is *what significance* such a theorist must attach to that fact when it comes to *evaluating conduct* in the context of those rules, for example, in determining how an official in such a system should behave.

A utilitarian or policy analyst might be thought to reason now as follows: "Institutions are justified if, or to the extent that, they promote human welfare or economic efficiency. Institutions ought to be designed so that official as well as private decisions will by and large promote such a value to the extent that this can be contrived. When that has been accomplished, conduct that is subject to the rules of those institutions can be justified only by reference to those rules. In other words, utilitarian and comparable arguments have their place, but they have no monopoly on justification. They do not always control the evaluation of conduct. When the rules are justified, they are to be followed. Their justified legal impact thus translates into moral force."

This is the approach John Rawls has suggested that a utilitarian would take to institutions that are justified on utilitarian grounds. In replying to the objection that utilitarianism allows the punishment of innocent persons, for example, he supposes that a utilitarian official who understands the utilitarian justification of the rules that he is charged with administering would abide by the rules.[8]

But the pattern of reasoning just sketched ignores some of the utilitarian considerations that are inevitably at work in particular cases that arise under such rules. For it is predictable that real social rules that are supported by the best utilitarian and economic arguments will require decisions in particular cases that would not most effectively promote welfare or efficiency. Such goals can sometimes be promoted more effectively by departing from the rules, or by changing them, than by following them. When that happens, a direct utilitarian or economic argument supports deviation from the rules.[9]

Suppose that a utilitarian official, or one who has adopted the precepts of normative economic analysis, is called upon to enforce the rules on

8. See John Rawls, "Two Concepts of Rules," *Philosophical Review* 64(1955): 3–32.

9. This point does not depart from the main thesis of *Forms and Limits of Utilitarianism,* in which I argued for the extensional equivalence of certain principles that I called "simple" and "general" utilitarianism. The extensional equivalence argument was extended to cover a limiting case of rule-utilitarianism—a theory (dubbed "primitive" rule-utilitarianism) in which no consideration is given to the complexity or cost of rules. Rule-utilitarian theories that concern themselves with ordinary, manageable social rules were explicitly excluded from the scope of that argument. Thus, *Forms and Limits of Utilitarianism* argues, in effect, that direct and indirect utilitarian arguments are *sometimes* equivalent. Along with this chapter, however, it assumes that they are *not always* equivalent.

Mary's behalf. He can understand perfectly the justification that he accepts for those rules. And his legal duty may be transparent. The rules vindicate Mary's claim, and he is legally bound to decide in her favor.

I do not see how such reasoning can settle matters for a utilitarian or economic-minded official. Suppose there are direct utilitarian or economic considerations on the other side—considerations sufficient to be appreciated by such officials, but not sufficient to surmount the justificatory threshold of Mary's rights. I do not see how our utilitarian or economic-minded official can regard these considerations as irrelevant to what he ought, ultimately, to do. He must regard them as providing arguments for deviating from existing rules, or for changing them, despite their justification. His primary aim, after all, is the promotion of welfare or efficiency. He must always consider arguments for promoting it directly, when he has the opportunity to do so. If so, he must be understood as prepared to violate Mary's legal rights—even though they are supposed to be morally defensible, from which it seems to follow that they have moral force and thus rule out unrestricted, direct, incremental utilitarian reasoning.

That is, a utilitarian official must be willing to reason as follows: "Mary's legal rights are clear, as is the utilitarian justification for allowing her to acquire such rights and to have them made enforceable by law. Even if this is an exceptional case, the same indirect utilitarian arguments continue to hold. Utilitarian legislators would be well advised not to modify the rules, should they have occasion to do so. These rules are as well designed, from a utilitarian standpoint, as any such rules can be. They cannot usefully be adjusted to take into account every special case that may arise under them. And, taking the utilitarian risks into account, it seems equally clear that welfare would be better served by not enforcing Mary's rights in this particular case." Acceptance of reasoning like this shows that such a theorist cannot fully accept the normative implications of his claim that Mary's legal rights are morally defensible. He cannot regard Mary's rights as making that difference to the evaluation of conduct that we supposed those rights do. For such reasoning cannot justify an infringement upon Mary's rights, though he is prepared to entertain it.

One might try to answer this objection in the following way: "An official who faces such a decision has more utilitarian reason to adhere to the rules than he has to depart from them. For an official who understands the utilitarian arguments for the rules appreciates that they assume general compliance on the part of officials as well as private citizens. This provides him with a general reason for believing that a departure from the rules is likely to do more harm than good. Furthermore, in any particular case it is likely that the direct utilitarian gains will be seen to be outweighed by the direct utilitarian costs of departing from the rules, resulting, for example, from frustrated expectations. It is therefore unreasonable to believe that a utilitarian official would depart from the rules instead of enforcing Mary's rights.''[10]

This argument requires that two points be made. In the first place, from the fact that a sound utilitarian argument is available for a legal rule it does not follow that utility will be maximized by adhering to the rules in each and every case. Conditions vary, and a sensitive utilitarian official will presumably be flexible. In the second place, the original argument can be understood as implying that officials *have an obligation* to comply with morally defensible rules that establish rights—an obligation that is not equivalent to the implications of direct utilitarian reasoning. Like Mary's rights, this obligation is not "absolute"; it can be overridden by substantial countervailing considerations. But, given Mary's rights and this corresponding obligation, direct, unrestricted, incremental utilitarian reasoning on the part of officials is ruled out. It is of course quite possible that direct utilitarian reasoning would yield conclusions that conform to Mary's rights; but this cannot be assumed. And the two modes of reasoning should not be confused.

A utilitarian might now reply in either of two ways. He might reject the pattern of reasoning that is entailed by talk of rights and obligations and maintain that we would be better off not to think in such terms. I do not address this issue here. My argument is meant to show certain difficulties that arise for utilitarian and comparable theories when they seek to *accommodate* rights (and obligations) under institutions they endorse.

Alternatively, a utilitarian might claim that a responsible utilitarian official would adopt a secondary principle (or perhaps a "rule of thumb") that requires him to adhere to the rules of utilitarian institutions. Such a principle, it may be said, is functionally equivalent to the

10. It seems to me that past critics of this section's argument failed to go significantly beyond reasoning like this paragraph's. See, e.g., Kent Greenwalt, ''Utilitarian Justifications for Observance of Legal Rights,'' and R. M. Hare, ''Utility and Rights: Comments on David Lyons's Essay—both in *Ethics, Economics, and the Law: Nomos XXIV,* ed. J. R. Pennock and J. W. Chapman (New York: New York University Press, 1982).

idea that an official is under an obligation to adhere to the rules and to respect the rights they confer.

This line of reasoning seems, however, to concede the point at issue. To make it plausible, one must suppose that experience demonstrates that utility is best served in the long run if one reasons just as if one was under such an obligation. But systematic evidence to this effect is rarely, if ever, offered. A utilitarian who argues in this way appreciates the force of the original objection but retains the hope of *somehow* finding utilitarian arguments to meet it. He offers us no more than a promissory note, without any assurance that it can be honored.

Bentham never faced this issue squarely, and I do not think that Mill did either. They seem to assume either that, once the rules are justified, they must be followed or else that particular cases simply cannot arise such that the justified rules require one thing and the direct application of the utilitarian standard to those cases requires another. Bentham and Mill were, perhaps, prevented from considering such difficulties by the assumption that, once justified rules are established, the legal recognition of the rights they confer change circumstances so that certain possible courses of action have added utility or disutility. Thus, it may be thought that there is always sufficient utilitarian reason of a direct kind to argue against deviation from justified rules. But this, as I have already suggested, cannot be assumed. Moreover, reasoning like this does not meet the point of the objection, which is that once those morally defensible rights are established, certain modes of reasoning are *illicit*.

Economists have not faced this issue squarely either. This is because they have not generally considered the implications of their economic "analysis" when it becomes a normative position. They are thus faced with a significant theoretical decision. Either they shall consider efficiency the sole fundamental basis for normative appraisals, of conduct as well as of institutions, in which case they must accept the consequences of the foregoing argument. Or they must accept the idea that there are other values to be served, beyond economic efficiency, in which case they must entertain the possibility of rights and obligations that are independent of social recognition and enforcement, rights and obligations that justified legal institutions ought to respect.

The problem I have sketched may be summarized as follows. Normative theories that are founded on certain values, such as welfare or efficiency, quite naturally regard legal rules or institutions as justified if they are supported by the best arguments in those terms. But such theories do not generate any obligation to adhere to the rules that they regard as justified. And they cannot do so unless they are restricted for just such a purpose.

The Relevance of Rule-Utilitarianism

A type of theory that might seem to meet this objection is rule-utilitarianism. In its relevant forms, rule-utilitarianism *limits* the application of the standard of utility to rules or social institutions and *requires compliance* with rules that are certified as having the requisite utilitarian justification. I do not mean to suggest that such a theory is incoherent. But, before proceeding further, we should distinguish two types of rule-utilitarian theory, only one of which is directly relevant to the present argument.

One type of rule-utilitarian theory seeks to accommodate the idea of moral obligations (and, derivatively, moral rights). It concerns itself with the "ideal moral rules" for a community or an "ideal moral code."[11] Another type of rule-utilitarian theory is concerned with established laws that can be defended on utilitarian grounds. It concerns itself with obligations to comply with useful social institutions. The latter, not the former, is most relevant here. For we are concerned with the question what difference it makes, from a moral point of view, to have laws and social institutions that are morally defensible. A rule-utilitarian of the first type does not address himself to this question, at least not in any direct way. But a rule-utilitarian of the second type in effect addresses himself to this question. This is the sort of rule-utilitarianism suggested (though not endorsed) by Rawls.[12]

My point about this sort of theory is that it represents a qualified utilitarian position. It does not follow from the more basic idea, common to all forms of utilitarianism, that human welfare is to be promoted. Nor does it follow from the more specific idea that social rules are to be evaluated in utilitarian terms.

What can be understood to follow from the fact that an institution can be supported by the best utilitarian arguments? If it follows that the rules

11. See, e.g., Richard B. Brandt, "Some Merits of One Form of Rule-Utilitarianism," *University of Colorado Studies Series in Philosophy* 1967: 39–65.

12. In John Rawls, "Two Concepts of Rules," *Philosophical Review* 64(1955): 3–32.

must be respected (or at least that there is a moral obligation to respect them), then the utilitarian has a basis for claiming that his theory accommodates legal rights with moral force. But not so otherwise. The question may be understood as follows. If a utilitarian believes that certain rules are justified on utilitarian grounds, does he *contradict* himself by supposing that direct utilitarian arguments for deviating from the rules may be entertained? I see no contradiction here; and in that case, the utilitarian cannot understand the legal impact of such rules automatically to translate into moral force, even when those rules are supported by the best utilitarian arguments. He cannot regard the morally defensible rights under *utilitarian* institutions as having moral force.

If so, the legal rights inclusion thesis must be qualified drastically, so that it becomes a morally uninteresting platitude. It cannot be understood to say that utilitarianism and comparable theories accommodate legal rights with their moral force intact, even when those rights are conferred by rules regarded as justified under such theories. It can be understood to say only that utilitarianism and comparable theories accept the possibility of justified institutions with rights that must be regarded as *merely* legal, devoid of moral force. For these theories do not allow the rights conferred by justified institutions to make the requisite difference to the evaluation of conduct that such rights are ordinarily assumed to do.

We can apply this to Rawls's argument, in which he suggested that a utilitarian official would abide by the rules of institutions he regarded as justified. We can understand Rawls's argument in either of two ways. He might be taken as suggesting that regarding rules as justified on utilitarian grounds *logically commits* one to abiding by their implications in particular cases. I have just tried to show that this is a mistake. Alternatively, Rawls might be understood as proposing that utilitarians *restrict their theory* so that it applies to rules or institutions but not to conduct under them. This is, I believe, a reasonable way of reading Rawl's suggestion, and the foregoing argument implies that it is the more generous of these two alternative readings.

For nothing in the idea that welfare is to be promoted restricts the application of the standard of utility to social rules or institutions. If such a restriction is *adopted* by a theorist who sees himself as working within the utilitarian tradition, that involves the *addition* of a factor that a utilitarian is not obliged to accept, either by the constraints of logic or by the normative implications of his theory. In the absence of such a factor, a utilitarian cannot ignore direct utilitarian arguments.

Imposing such a restriction on the idea that human welfare is to be promoted is either arbitrary or else motivated by a desire to accommodate the moral force of rights and obligations under justified rules. In its relevant forms, rule-utilitarianism represents a compromise—a recognition that the utilitarian approach is incomplete at best and, unless it is restricted, cannot accommodate the moral force of morally defensible legal rights and obligations.

Similar considerations apply to normative theories based on the goal of economic efficiency. If the moral force of legal rights and obligations under justified institutions is to be accommodated, then those theories must be restricted. And restricting them reopens general questions about the standards to be used in evaluating institutions themselves.

It may be thought that I have overstated my case. I have suggested that a utilitarian (unless he restricts his theory to accommodate objections) will evaluate conduct by means of direct utilitarian considerations—in effect, by act-utilitarian reasoning. But, it may be objected, from the fact that an institution is supported by the best utilitarian arguments it must be thought by a utilitarian to follow that one has reason to conform to the rules of that institution. I have ignored, it may be said, the direct practical implications that the utilitarian justification of social rules or institutions has for a utilitarian.

If this were correct, then the most that could be claimed is that utilitarianism gives rise in such contexts to *conflicting* considerations. The foregoing reasoning would not show that direct utilitarian arguments concerning conduct are *excluded* by a utilitarian justification of the institutions within the context of which that conduct may take place. It would show only that such arguments must be weighed within utilitarianism against arguments flowing from the utilitarian justification of those institutions. Then the most that could be said for utilitarianism is either that one who follows its dictates would not violate the rights it regards as justified as often as my argument implies (though he would violate them sometimes) or else that utilitarianism is indeterminate in such cases, in which event it would not require that such rights as it regards as morally defensible ought to be respected.

If they are sound, such consequences cannot offer much comfort to the utilitarian. But are they sound? I think not. To see this, we must distinguish between (1) a reason for maintaining an institution and (2) a reason for conforming to institutional rules. It is reasonable to suppose that the utilitarian justification of an institution provides a utilitarian with a reason of type (1), that is, a reason for maintaining that institution. But we cannot assume that a reason of type (2) likewise follows. The utilitarian justification of an institution provides a reason for conforming to that institution *only if* conformity to its rules is required, in the circumstances, for maintaining that institution. But this is just what we cannot assume. For it is possible for the rules to be violated (by officials or private individuals) without threatening the institution—more precisely, without threatening its utility. In such a case, the utilitarian justification of the institution provides the utilitarian himself with no reason for conforming to its rules—not when greater utility accrues to deviation from them.

Someone might approach this issue differently. One reason why indirect utilitarian considerations, concerning rules and institutions, do not converge with direct utilitarian considerations, concerning individuals' conduct, is that real social rules must be simple enough for the practical guidance of ordinary mortals and also typically involve social costs. These costs include sanctions designed to coerce officials and private individuals into following the law when they may be tempted to act otherwise. A person might therefore reason that an official would be strongly constrained to follow rules that are predicated upon serving human welfare when those rules have been properly designed. One might suppose that a utilitarian institution would be contrived so as to make it very undesirable for an official to depart from rules that he is charged with administering. Useful sanctions might seem to insure that Mary's rights would be respected.

But we cannot assume that such expedients will do the trick. In the first place, we cannot assume that maximally useful rules, or rules supported by the best utilitarian arguments, would always be sufficiently constraining to prevent deviation from them. In the second place, someone who is guided by utilitarian considerations should not be influenced so decisively by considerations of self-interest as this suggestion assumes. He should be willing to accept a risk himself, for the sake of serving the *general* welfare more effectively, as the direct utilitarian arguments that counsel infringements on Mary's rights show possible.

Alternatively, one might assume that an official would not deviate from rules that he is charged with administering, because he would think it *wrong* to do so. One might suppose, for example, that an official would regard himself as having accepted a position of public trust, which involves obligations that he cannot in good conscience ignore. He might see himself as morally bound by his commitment to adhere to the rules as he finds them. But, if we suppose that such a factor is at work in our example, then we are assuming, in effect, the influence of *non*-utilitarian arguments. If the argument suggested here is to make any difference, it must be based on the idea of an independent obligation that does not follow from the considerations already canvassed. To have recourse to such obligations, however, is to concede that utilitarian principles need supplementation before we can secure a normative theory that is capable of accommodating ordinary legal rights with moral force.

Extension of the Argument

As we have already observed, this argument would not seem limited to utilitarianism, but concerns also the relationship of rights to other closely related theories, such as economic analysis when offered as a normative approach to law or social policy. But the considerations that extend the argument *that* far suggest that it must extend much further.[13] The argument would seem to concern all "goal-based" theories that satisfy two conditions: (1) the goal or goals accepted by the theory as the basis for appraising institutions are capable of being served not only through institutional design but also by the actions of individuals when their conduct falls under the scope of the institutional rules; and (2) the goal or goals do not (separately or together) entail some value that demands respect for rules that are favorably appraised in relation to them. The latter condition is vague, and I am not sure what sort of goal might fail to meet it. It simply seems necessary to allow that some goals might satisfy condition (1) but would also require respect for the rights conferred by institutions that serve those goals, in the way that welfare, happiness, economic efficiency, and the like do not.

To illustrate the way the argument might be extended, imagine that we dedicate a legal system to the service of social and economic equality—a useful example, since this value is often contrasted with

13. I owe this suggestion to Jules Coleman.

utility and is believed to conflict with the latter in practice. The same sorts of problems concerning rights accrue to a theory based on promoting substantive equality as attach to one based on human welfare or economic efficiency. For the rules of institutions might be contrived to serve social and economic equality as far as it is possible for rules to do, but it would still be possible for social and economic equality to be served (perhaps in small ways) by deviation from those rules in particular cases. There is nothing about the basic value to be served that requires respect for all the rights that may be conferred by such institutions.

If we explored this issue further, we might find that a very wide range of goal-based normative theories have the same trouble with legal rights. We might also find that other sorts of theories (e.g., "right-based" and "duty-based" theories) face similar difficulties.

What all of this seems to show is that normative theories require a more complex character than those we have considered if they are to accommodate the moral force of legal rights under justified institutions. Many theories fail to account for an obligation to adhere to rules that are regarded by them as justified. From the assumption that rules serve appropriate values it does not seem to follow that there is the requisite sort of obligation to adhere to them, an obligation that gives due respect to the morally defensible rights conferred by those rules.

If a utilitarian (or other goal-based) theory of *moral* obligations were possible, it might fill the gap just noted. It might explain how we have moral obligations to comply with social institutions that are predicated on serving the general welfare, for example. We cannot assume that a utilitarian theory of moral obligations would generate precisely this obligation, but the possibility of a normative utilitarian theory of legal rights would be revived.

This development is ironic, for it rests the possibility of a normative theory of *legal* rights upon the possibility of a theory of *moral* obligations, though the former is usually thought to be much less problematic than the latter. In any case, it brings us round full circle. We began by noting the traditional utilitarian attitude toward moral rights, embraced by Bentham, which is similar to the traditional utilitarian attitude toward moral obligations (when obligations are not confused with whatever happens to be required by some sort of normative principle). Like rights, obligations have a normative life of their own, with implications that are neither reducible to, nor traceable by, direct considerations of utility. It does not follow, however, that a utilitarian theory of moral rights or obligations is impossible.

Mill's Theory of Moral Rights and Obligations

In previous works I have offered a sympathetic reading of Mill's theory of morality and justice, in order to challenge the usual view that utilitarianism is incapable of accommodating either moral rights or moral obligations. (In recent years emphasis has been placed on rights, but in the first half of this century obligations received similar attention.) I would like now to summarize that argument briefly and show why it seems to fail. Considerations relevant to the main argument, concerning legal rights, apply here too.

Mill's theory is promising because (under the interpretation I have offered) his way of trying to accommodate moral rights and obligations is not a form of ad hoc revisionism motivated by the desire to evade substantive objections to utilitarianism. It is not a form of revisionism at all, but turns on a theory of the moral concepts, the relations among which establish constraints upon any normative theory. Instead of adopting (what has since been thought of as) the standard utilitarian approach to moral reasoning—instead of assuming that one is always required to promote a certain value to the maximum degree possible—Mill begins by sketching a stratified analysis of normative concepts.

Mill's general idea can be understood as follows. We can distinguish three levels of normative concepts and judgments. For present purposes, the bottom (most concrete) level concerns the rightness or wrongness, justice or injustice, morality or immorality of particular acts. The intermediate, second level consists of moral principles, which concern (general) moral rights and obligations. Judgments of right and wrong conduct at the bottom level are functions of moral rights and obligations, and of nothing else. (Since moral rights are assumed to be correlative to obligations, but not vice versa, this can be put solely in terms of obligations.) A particular act is right if and only if it does not breach a moral obligation, unless that obligation has been overridden by another obligation. But moral principles are not self-certifying; they turn upon values they somehow serve (Mill is least clear about this relation). The topmost level of normative judgments and concepts concerns the values that may be invoked to establish moral principles (which concern general moral rights and obligations). For Mill, of course, the value at work at this topmost level is human happiness or welfare. So, moral principles about general rights and obligations are supposed to have a direct relationship to the principle of utility. But judgments concerning the rightness or wrongness of particular actions have *no* such relation. Acts must be judged as right or wrong depending on whether they respect moral rights and obligations, and *never* on the basis of direct utilitarian reasoning.

This feature of Mill's reconstructed analytic theory is vital to the possibility of a utilitarian account of moral rights and obligations. It insures that Mill's theory does not collapse into act-utilitarianism. It insures, more generally, that the evaluation of conduct in his theory is not dominated by direct utilitarian considerations. Mill's way of insuring this is by conceptual analysis, which leads to the claim that moral concepts are so stratified that interactions are possible between adjacent levels but are absolutely prohibited between the top and bottom levels. Without this conceptual foundation, his theory would either collapse into act-utilitarianism or amount to just another, more or less arbitrary, revision of utilitarianism.

Mill's conceptual claims provide a necessary (though not a sufficient) condition for accommodating moral rights and obligations, if we assume that moral rights and obligations possess normative force (which Mill suggests). In the present context, that makes possible the hope that his theory will generate a moral obligation to conform to the actual rules of institutions that can be defended on utilitarian grounds, so that the theory will require respect for the rights conferred by such rules.

The success of Mill's theory thus turns upon the truth of his conceptual claims. But these seem stronger than the moral concepts can bear. It is plausible to hold that what is right or wrong is at least in part a function of moral rights and obligations (this is what is meant by the normative force of moral rights and obligations). But it is not so plausible to hold that the concepts involved *completely prohibit* the direct appeal to ultimate values, such as human welfare, when evaluating conduct. On the view I have ascribed to Mill—the one that promises a way of accommodating moral rights and obligations—someone who evaluates conduct by means of direct utilitarian arguments is guilty of a conceptual mistake. He is not reasoning unsoundly; he is reasoning *fallaciously*. But this appears excessive, to say the least; and yet nothing short of this will secure Mill's moral principles from being dominated by direct utilitarian considerations.

Consider, for example, our imaginary utilitarian official. When he takes into account the effects of his conduct on human welfare while trying to decide what to do, he does not seem to be confused or to be violating the constraints of the moral concepts. If he places too much weight upon direct utilitarian considerations, that may be a moral error, but it does not look like a conceptual mistake. As a utilitarian, it seems incumbent on him to consider the effects of his conduct on welfare. If so, we have no reason to believe that direct utilitarian considerations will not dominate his moral reasoning. Thus, we have no reason to believe that a satisfactory utilitarian theory of *moral* rights and obligations can be developed. So we have no reason to believe that a utilitarian would be obliged to respect the moral force of justified *legal* rights and obligations.

Summary

A utilitarian might be assumed to reason as follows: "I will have no truck with 'moral rights,' which are figments of unenlightened moralists' imaginations. I am concerned with human welfare, with promoting it as far as possible, and I approve of social institutions to the extent they serve that purpose. Those institutions are morally defensible, and no others are. Under them, people have rights—not imaginary, toothless rights, but real, enforceable rights."

This was Bentham's attitude (though not Mill's), and it fits the normative thinking found most generally in the literature of "economic analysis." The trouble is, it ignores a central normative issue, what conduct is required or permitted by the theory that endorses those allegedly justifiable rights.

Economists might be excused for neglecting this issue (at least until it is pointed out to them), since they tend to think only about rules and regulations and to ignore how principles apply directly to individuals' conduct—perhaps because they have not approached their normative conclusions from a self-consciously normative standpoint. But utilitarians have no such excuse. As Bentham was aware, the aim of promoting some value like human welfare is as relevant to individual acts as it is to social institutions; the latter application does not rule out the former. But, unless utilitarianism is restricted, its direct application to conduct undermines respect for the very rights it wishes to endorse.

Bibliography

Bentham, Jeremy. "Anarchical Fallacies." In *The Works of Jeremy Bentham,* ed. J. Bowring, 2: 489–534. Edinburgh: Tait, 1838–43.

———. "A General View of a Complete Code of Laws." In *The Works of Jeremy Bentham,* ed. J. Bowring, 3: 155–210. Edinburgh: Tait, 1838–43.

———. "Pannomial Fragments." In *The Works of Jeremy Bentham,* ed. J. Bowring, 3: 211–30. Edinburgh: Tait, 1838–43.

Berger, Fred R. *Happiness, Justice, and Freedom: The Moral and Political Philosophy of John Stuart Mill.* Berkeley: University of California Press, 1984.

———. "John Stuart Mill on Justice and Fairness." In *New Essays on John Stuart Mill and Utilitarianism,* ed. W. E. Cooper, K. Nielsen, and S. C. Patten. *Canadian Journal of Philosophy Suppl.* 5(1979): 115–36.

Brandt, Richard B. "Some Merits of One Form of Rule-Utilitarianism." *University of Colorado Studies, Series in Philosophy* 1967: 39–65.

———. "A Utilitarian Theory of Excuses." *Philosophical Review* 68(1969): 337–61.

———. "Utilitarianism and Moral Rights." *Canadian Journal of Philosophy* 14(1984): 1–19.

Brink, David O. "Mill's Deliberative Utilitarianism." *Philosophy and Public Affairs* 21(1992): 67–103.

Brown, D. G. "Mill on Liberty and Morality." *Philosophical Review* 81(1972): 133–58.

———. "Mill's Act-Utilitarianism." *Philosophical Quarterly* 24(1974): 67–68.

———. "What Is Mill's Principle of Utility?" *Canadian Journal of Philosophy* 3(1973): 1–12.

Calebresi, Guido, and A. Douglas Melamed. "Property Rules, Liability Rules, and Inalienability: One View of the Cathedral.'' *Harvard Law Review* 85(1972): 1089–1128.

Card, Claudia. ''Utility and the Basis of Moral Rights: A Reply to R. B. Brandt.'' *Canadian Journal of Philosophy* 14(1984): 21–30.

Copp, David. ''The Iterated Utilitarianism of J. S. Mill.'' In *New Essays on John Stuart Mill and Utilitarianism,* ed. W. E. Cooper, K. Nielsen, and S. C. Patten. *Canadian Journal of Philosophy Suppl.* 5(1979): 75–98.

Cupples, Brian. ''A Defense of the Received Interpretation of J. S. Mill.'' *Australasian Journal of Philosophy* 50(1972): 131–37.

Dryer, D. P. ''Justice, Liberty, and the Principle of Utility in Mill.'' In *New Essays on John Stuart Mill and Utilitarianism,* ed. W. E. Cooper, K. Nielsen, and S. C. Patten. *Canadian Journal of Philosophy Suppl.* 5(1979): 63–73.

―――. ''Mill's Utilitarianism.'' In *Essays on Ethics, Religion, and Society,* ed. J. M. Robson. The Collected Works of John Stuart Mill, 10: lxiii–cxiii. Toronto: University of Toronto Press, 1969.

Dworkin, Ronald M. *Law's Empire.* Cambridge: Harvard University Press, 1986.

―――. '''Natural' Law Revisited.'' *University of Florida Law Review* 34(1982): 165–88.

―――. *Taking Rights Seriously.* Cambridge: Harvard University Press, 1978.

Feinberg, Joel. ''Duties, Rights, and Claims.'' *American Philosophical Quarterly* 3(1966): 137–42.

―――. *Freedom and Fulfillment: Philosophical Essays.* Princeton: Princeton University Press, 1992.

―――. ''Justice and Personal Desert.'' In *Justice: Nomos VI,* ed. C. J. Friedrich and J. W. Chapman, pp. 69–97. New York: Leiber–Atherton, 1974.

―――. ''Noncomparative Justice.'' *Philosophical Review* 83(1974): 297–338.

―――. *Social Philosophy.* Englewood Cliffs, N.J.: Prentice–Hall, 1973.

Flathman, Richard E. ''Rights, Utility, and Civil Disobedience.'' In *Ethics, Economics, and the Law: Nomos XXIV,* ed. J. R. Pennock and J. W. Chapman, pp. 194–209. New York: New York University Press, 1982.

Fletcher, George. ''Utility and Skepticism.'' In *Ethics, Economics, and the Law: Nomos XXIV,* ed. J. R. Pennock and J. W. Chapman, pp. 210–15. New York: New York University Press, 1982.

Gewirth, Alan. ''Can Utilitarianism Justify Any Moral Rights?'' In *Ethics, Economics, and the Law: Nomos XXIV,* ed. J. R. Pennock and J. W. Chapman, pp 158–91. New York: New York University Press, 1982.

Gibbard, Allan. ''Utilitarianism and Human Rights.'' *Social Philosophy and Policy* 1(1984):92–102.

Gray, John. ''Indirect Utility and Fundamental Rights.'' *Social Philosophy and Policy* 1(1984): 73–91.

―――. *Mill on Liberty: A Defence.* London: Routledge and Kegan Paul, 1983.

Greenawalt, Kent. "Utilitarian Justifications for Observance of Legal Rights." In *Ethics, Economics, and the Law: Nomos XXIV*, ed. J. R. Pennock and J. W. Chapman, pp. 139–47. New York: New York University Press, 1982.

Hare, R. M. "Utility and Rights: Comment on David Lyons's Essay." In *Ethics, Economics, and the Law: Nomos XXIV*, ed. J. R. Pennock and J. W. Chapman, pp. 148–57. New York: New York University Press, 1982.

Harrison, Jonathan. "The Expedient, the Right, and the Just in Mill's *Utilitarianism*." *Canadian Journal of Philosophy Suppl.* 1, pt. 1(1974): 93–107.

Hart, H. L. A. "Are There Any Natural Rights?" *Philosophical Review* 64(1955): 175–91.

———. "Bentham: Lecture on a Master Mind." *Proceedings of the British Academy* 48(1962): 197–320.

———. "Bentham on Legal Rights." In *Oxford Essays in Jurisprudence: Second Series,* ed. A. W. B. Simpson, pp. 171–201. Oxford: Clarendon, 1973.

———. *The Concept of Law.* Oxford: Clarendon, 1961.

———. *Definition and Theory in Jurisprudence.* Oxford: Clarendon, 1953.

———. *Essays on Bentham: Jurisprudence and Legal Theory.* Oxford: Clarendon, 1982.

———. "Legal and Moral Obligation." In *Essays in Moral Philosophy,* ed. A. I. Melden, pp. 82–107. Seattle: University of Washington Press, 1958.

———. "Positivism and the Separation of Law and Morals." *Harvard Law Review* 71(1958): 593–629.

Hohfeld, Wesley Newcomb. *Fundamental Legal Conceptions as Applied in Judicial Reasoning.* Ed. W. W. Cook. New Haven: Yale University Press, 1964.

Lyons, David. *Forms and Limits of Utilitarianism.* Oxford: Clarendon, 1965.

———. "Human Rights and the General Welfare." *Philosophy and Public Affairs* 6(1977): 113–29.

———. *In the Interest of the Governed: A Study in Bentham's Philosophy of Utility and Law.* Rev. ed. Oxford: Clarendon, 1991.

———. "On Formal Justice." *Cornell Law Review* 58(1973): 833–61.

———. Review of *H.L.A. Hart,* by Neil MacCormick. *Cornell Law Review* 68(1983): 257–68.

———. "Utility as a Possible Ground of Rights." *Noûs* 14(1980): 17–28.

Mabbott, J. D. "Interpretations of Mill's *Utilitarianism*." *Philosophical Quarterly* 6(1956): 115–120.

MacCormick, D. N. "Rights in Legislation." In *Law, Morality, and Society: Essays in Honour of H.L.A. Hart,* ed. P. M. S. Hacker and J. Raz, pp. 189–209. Oxford: Clarendon, 1977.

Mandelbaum, Maurice. "Two Moot Issues in Mill's *Utilitarianism.*" In *Mill*, ed. J. B. Schneewind, pp. 206–33. Garden City: Doubleday, 1968.

Mill, John Stuart. "Remarks on Bentham's Philosophy." In *Essays on Ethics, Religion, and Society*, ed. J. M. Robson. *The Collected Works of John Stuart Mill*, 10: 5–18. Toronto: University of Toronto Press, 1969.

Nozick, Robert. "Distributive Justice." *Philosophy and Public Affairs* 3(1973): 45–126.

Ogden, C. K. *Bentham's Theory of Fictions*. Patterson, N.J.: Littlefield, Adams, 1959.

Pettit, Philip. "The Consequentialist Can Recognise Rights." *Philosophical Quarterly* 38(1988): 42–53.

Posner, Richard A. "Utilitarianism, Economics, and Legal Theory." *Journal of Legal Studies* 8(1979): 103–40.

Quinton, Anthony. *Utilitarian Ethics*. London: Macmillan, 1973.

Rawls, John. "Justice as Fairness," *Philosophical Review* 67(1958): 179–83.

———. *A Theory of Justice*. Cambridge, Mass.: Belknap, 1971.

———. "Two Concepts of Rules." *Philosophical Review* 64(1955):3–32.

Raz, Joseph. *The Morality of Freedom*. Oxford: Clarendon, 1986.

———. *Practical Reason and Norms*. 2d ed. Princeton University Press, 1990.

Ross, W. D. *The Right and the Good*. Oxford: Clarendon, 1930.

Ryan, Alan. *The Philosophy of John Stuart Mill*. 2d ed. Atlantic Highlands, N.J.: Humanities, 1990.

Salmond, John W. *Salmond on Jurisprudence*. 11th ed. Ed. G. Williams. London: Sweet & Maxwell, 1957.

Scanlon, T. M. "Rights, Goals, and Fairness." *Erkenntnis* 2(1977): 81–94.

Schneewind, Jerome. "A Note on Promising." *Philosophical Studies* 17(1966):33–35.

Sosa, Ernest. "Mill's *Utilitarianism.*" In *Mill's Utilitarianism*, ed. J. M. Smith and E. Sosa, pp. 154–72. Belmont, Calif.: Wadsworth, 1969.

Sumner, L. W. "The Good and the Right." In *New Essays on John Stuart Mill and Utilitarianism*, ed. W. E. Cooper, K. Nielsen, and S. C. Patten. *Canadian Journal of Philosophy Suppl.* 5(1979): 99–114.

———. *The Moral Foundation of Rights*. Oxford: Clarendon, 1987.

———. "Rights Denaturalized." In *Utility and Rights*, ed. R. G. Frey, pp. 20–41. Minneapolis: University of Minnesota Press, 1984.

Ten, C. L. *Mill on Liberty*. Oxford: Clarendon, 1980.

Thomson, Judith Jarvis. *The Realm of Rights*. Cambridge: Harvard University Press, 1990.

Urmson, J. O. "The Interpretation of the Moral Philosophy of J. S. Mill." *Philosophical Quarterly* 3(1953): 33–39.

Wellman, Carl. *A Theory of Rights: Persons Under Laws, Institutions, and Morals*. Totowa, N.J.: Rowman & Allanheld, 1985.

Index